The Creation of United States
Air Power for World War II

theDragon'sTeeth?

Benjamin S. Kelsey
Brigadier General
United States Air Force (Ret.)

Smithsonian Institution Press
Washington, D.C. • 1982

All photographs are from the files of the
National Air and Space Museum.

Library of Congress Cataloging in Publication Data

Kelsey, Benjamin S., d. 1981

The dragon's teeth?

Includes index.
Supt. of Docs. no.: SI 1.2:D78

1. United States. Army. Air Corps—History. I. Title.

UG633.K43 1982   358.4'00973   82-600279

ISBN 0-87474-574-8

The Creation of United States
Air Power
for World War II

Benjamin S. Kelsey
Brigadier General
United States Air Force (Ret.)

theDragon'sTeeth?

DEDICATION

To the memory of OLIVER P. ECHOLS, Major General, United States Air Force, whose influence over so many years permeated so many facets of the development, production, and distribution of the aircraft for the Second World War that he might be called "The Man Who Won World War II." Without his wisdom, courage, and inspirational guidance, the weapons that the combat crews used would have been fewer and less potent. The respect that he enjoyed from the aircraft industry, Congress, his superiors, and most of all from his subordinates was due primarily to his impeccable integrity.

IN MEMORIAM

Brigadier General Benjamin S. Kelsey (USAF, Ret.) died on March 3, 1981, after a long and distinguished career. He was a crucial force in developing United States air power in the years preceding World War II, serving as chief of the Fighter Project Branch at Wright Field in the 1930s. During the war, he was deputy chief of staff of the Ninth Fighter Command in England and, later, chief of the Operational Engineering Section of the Eighth Air Force. After his retirement in 1955, Kelsey continued to teach and write about aeronautical matters. At the time of his death, he was finishing The Dragon's Teeth?, *which he wrote as the occupant of the Charles A. Lindbergh Chair of Aerospace History of the National Air and Space Museum.*

theDragon'sTeeth?

CONTENTS

FOREWORD

According to myth, the Phoenician prince Cadmus threw a set of dragon's teeth onto a plowed field, and a host of warriors sprang up fully armed. The instantaneous response, complete with weapons, makes it a myth. The creation of U.S. air power for World War II, although almost as incredible, was no myth; the time and weapons were real. Cold facts reveal numbers and time, but the seeds were planted and the tenuous growth nurtured for years before the response was needed.

Even for those individuals who were involved at the time, it is difficult to appreciate fully either the meager base from which the expansion took place or the magnitude of the final effort. The aircraft industry, supported by both civil and military procurement, had almost no civil output from 1919 to about 1926. Military production averaged about 450 aircraft a year, with a low point of 226 in 1922—hardly enough to maintain a viable industry. Beginning in 1927, probably spurred by Lindbergh's flight, America's civilian requirements increased and supported a minimal productive capacity, but even this activity was short-lived.

From 1932 to 1935, the total production of both civilian and military planes dropped to about half what it had been from 1927 to 1931. For the military, the low point came in 1934, when only 437 planes were built. The average for 1933–35 was only 450 planes per year, about the same as it had been since World War I. This period of two or three years during the Depression was the base from which the expansion to World War II aircraft types and production had to spring.

Military production of 437 planes in 1934 became 96,318 in 1944, a 220-fold increase in ten years. From 1940 to 1945, some 330,000 military planes were produced. It is little wonder that the word *miraculous* is frequently used in accounts of the expansion process.

The figures are only an inkling of *what* happened. The *how* and *why* are more important. Even the myth allowed for some factors other than simply throwing a handful of teeth onto a plowed field. Cadmus had to get guidance from the oracle to know where to find the dragon and what to do with it. Then he had to slay the dragon and extract its teeth, both of which seemed to be formidable tasks, but the manner of the accomplishment is left to the imagination. The presence of a conveniently plowed field in which to throw the teeth is pure mythical privilege.

The antipathy for all things military and the apathy with which the country viewed the rise of the totalitarian threat constituted a symbolic dragon. The concept of air power seemed to be a dream, a myth, kept alive by an unrecognized and largely unrespected few. Not only was the ground upon which the expansion had to take place unprepared, but to many of us it seemed to be a wasteland of frustration and futility.

By the time Japan surrendered on August 14, 1945, about half the nation's total effort was being expended to support the war. About 20 percent of the total U.S. dollars spent for war went for aircraft and their use. Thus, it is hard to picture the tenuous effort and small number of people that sustained the potential for creating this force during the preceding decade.

Where the myth says that a fully armed host of warriors sprang up from the dragon's teeth, reality parts dramatically. Our preparedness seems to assume the character of the myth in presuming that an armed force can be called into being whenever needed *after* an emergency. Reality demands a lead time for the creation of arms, for the organization and training of the force, and even for the development of doctrine for their use.

The 1930s merit reviewing because they hold clues to how America's fantastic military performance was achieved. The decade also provides sober warnings to those who prefer myth to reality and illustrates the difficult compromises that must be made between preparedness and the economic, social, and political pressures that are always with us.

No single volume can explain all the facets of the situation, nor can any single viewpoint be considered completely objective. However, it is difficult to evaluate the factual data without some personal insight. There were many differences of opinion at the time, and there will be many differences in the appraisals and conclusions now.

Many of the considerations pertinent to the Air Corps applied to the Navy, civil aviation, and the aviation industry, and several of these can only be developed from their point of reference. This is particularly true of the people involved and their working relations. I hope that others will amplify my treatment here with material relating more specifically to the Navy, the aviation industry, and civil aviation.

Though this book is not a narration of personal recollections, some of its illustrations inevitably must come from personal experience. To this extent, some bias is readily acknowledged. However, in order to preserve a "how it looked from here" aspect, the normal historical research approach has been modified. A draft was prepared in nearly complete form, using reference material only for dates and numbers. Subsequent reference was made to other sources to confirm or refute the author's convictions or impressions. Wherever possible, interviews with other involved individuals have been used to amplify or correct the original draft.

A common experience of the participants at the time of the air power buildup was that much of the basis for their decision making was not recorded, being based on informal communication. In part, this intimate relationship accounted for expediting action and getting things done with minimum resources. When some of these individuals were asked recently "How did so few people get so much done with so little to work with?" the answer in each case was "Because there were so few people."

It was impossible to make desired decisions, not only in the period of expansion, but also throughout the previous period of scarcity. There was never enough money to maintain a military force, let alone to modernize it. The number of boards, committees, and investigations conducted during the 1920s and the 1930s must have reached a hundred or more. They universally stressed the existing lack of force necessary for minimum security, the obsolescence of equipment, and an industrial base that was deplorably inadequate for mobilization.

In reviewing *what* happened regarding statistics, weapons performance, the numbers and allocations of people, and time, the universally important element is time. Time to develop technology and doctrine, time to create capability to produce, time to build equipment and force are all real factors. But superimosed is the time to develop sufficient support from enough people to insure a self-sustaining effort. This may be likened to the "critical mass" in atomic reaction, where enough elemental units have to become involved to make the reaction self-supporting. In the 1920s and 1930s, it was evident that tomorrow was ten years off. When all the elements seemed to be in place for immediately taking off on a new program, it inevitably took about ten years for the reality to appear. As this is being written in 1979, it appears that tomorrow is more nearly twenty years off. This, due to more people and the greater complexity of distracting influences, makes the problem of security at once more difficult and more urgent.

If it is not already apparent, the reason for examining this period is that the fundamental problem of mobilization potential is always present from generation to generation. The period of the 1920s and 1930s is but one example, although a vivid one, of a situation that recurs periodically.

This greatest mobilization effort in our history was particularly revealing in the circumstances pertaining to air power. The starting base was small, the doctrine was untried, the weapons were only just developing, and the results were overwhelming. Nevertheless, the lessons seem not to have been appreciated. The United States has been faced with two similar situations of smaller magnitude, Korea and Vietnam. There is some evidence that the cycle is occurring again.

Because of the small number of people participating in the effort of the 1930s, the records tend to be deficient. This may have obscured the lessons contained in the experience. It seems worthwhile to examine the era again from a fresh point of view.

A common misinterpretation is that the active military force should be responsive to an estimate of the existing threat. It should more nearly be determined by the efficient distribution and use of *our own* resources. Only a dictator with aggressive aims can create and maintain a force appropriate to, and adequate for, a specific campaign. Specific measures to counter a specific threat will almost automatically guarantee that if an emergency occurs it will be in a different place and of a different nature.

All through the following pages, there is an underlying theme, either directly stated or implied, that the proper size of a military force in-being is one that, for its training, maintenance, and replacement keeps alive a base for expansion to whatever level may be critically required.

PREFACE

I first met Ben Kelsey at MIT during the mid-1920s. Ben was an undergraduate, still in his teens, but it was already clear that he had the makings of an extraordinary airman. He taught himself to fly at age 14 and brought a considerable fund of experience in the air to the solution of classroom engineering problems. Over the next half-century, he more than fulfilled that early promise.

Having known Ben, I was particularly pleased to learn that the Army had assigned him as my safety pilot during the first blind-flying demonstrations conducted for the Guggenheim Fund for the Promotion of Aeronautics in 1929. From the start, he was a full-fledged member of the team and did much of the experimental work. His piloting help, criticisms of the test carried out, and sound technical counsel contributed greatly to the results achieved.

Ben's pleasant personality, his wit, and that ever-present lopsided grin are among my most pleasant memories of the period. He helped keep things in perspective. We made the first "official under-the-hood" blind flight in the presence of Daniel Guggenheim and other distinguished observers on the morning of September 24, 1929. Ben was fully prepared, in his words, "to grab the stick if it got too dangerous."

I had already made a series of textbook approaches and landings, but not this time. Despite all my previous practice, and a solo blind landing in dense fog earlier that morning, the approach and landing were sloppy. I was annoyed, but Ben saw the humor in the situation. I might also add that he never let me forget bouncing the airplane in front of Mr. Guggenheim and the assembled officials.

Ben remained at the center of research and development in military aeronautics for the rest of his career. During the thin years of the Depression, he was one of the small band of enthusiasts, many of them underpaid lieutenants and captains, who sought to spend those precious few tax dollars allocated to the Air Corps in the wisest possible fashion. Few men had a better understanding of the joint problems of research and development and of aircraft procurement than Ben Kelsey had. He was a tireless worker who combined a very clear vision of the requirements that would have to be met in the next war with the drive, courage, and know-how to ensure that the American air weapon would be there when it was needed.

We owe an enormous debt to Ben Kelsey and others like him who fought public indifference and official apathy to the needs of airpower. The great fighter aircraft of World War II were a part of Ben's legacy to the nation. His understanding of the need for preparedness and his unique ability to draw lessons for the future from the experience of the past may represent an even more important bequest, however. This book is a distillation of the experience of his generation of American airmen. It deserves to be read and understood by a new generation of Americans who cannot afford to forget the lessons Ben Kelsey sought to teach.

—J. H. Doolittle (Lt. Gen., USAF, Ret.)

I THE CRITICAL CHALLENGE

During the latter stages of World War II, the huge plant built by Bell Aircraft for constructing B-29s at Marietta, Georgia, was just starting production. Although a production rate of seventy planes a month was eventually reached, the start-up pains were intense. Harvey Gaylord says that he was in a conference one evening in Carl Cover's office attended by a number of department heads who were reviewing the day's production problems. Gaylord had been a key member of the Bell organization over the years, and Cover was the plant manager at the time. During the agonizing discussion, an office attendant, recruited from the local unskilled labor pool, seriously suggested, "Mr. Cover, you're having so many problems making those bombers why don't you just go out and buy them instead of going to all this trouble?"

This incident illustrates a point of view held by too many people before, during, and after the war—"Why didn't they . . . ?" The answer then, and now, had to be that the facilities, resources, and people were not available to permit some of the most desirable choices.

There were really three parts to the problem. One was the limited production base that had existed all during the Depression. Another was the restricted support given to development during the period due to the urgent social and economic demands of the general public. A third difficulty was the conflict within and between the services and in the higher echelons of government over the proper role of aircraft.

THE ELEMENT OF TIME

As always, running through all the technical and economic considerations was the element of time. Urgency, money, and intense effort can compress time only so much until an irreducible minimum is met. It takes time—"lead time" to create designs and test articles and "make-ready time" to build the production capability necessary for producing large numbers of aircraft. Although foresight and awareness should provide some help, these qualities are always in short supply. The interplay of extraneous factors existing then, notably the early purchases by the English and French, reduced somewhat the impact of time, but it would be folly to expect similar factors to be helpful to the same degree in another situation.

One economic study concluded that in the first two years of United States involvement in the war, the industrial plant of the nation, exclusive of Navy yards and Army arsenals, was doubled. When one considers that whatever industrial capacity existed after generations of creation was duplicated in such a short time, it is apparent that a tremendous effort was expended just to build up a potential capability, let alone build the matériel of war. It makes little difference what the estimated value of the plant was or whether it took more or less time than the estimated two years. The point is simply that all decisions and efforts were influenced by the need to do *something else first*.

For air power, the situation was intensified. The capital plant and skilled manpower pool had suffered from near starvation for better than a decade. Perhaps a conversation with Robert Gross, president of Lockheed, about 1939, standing outside the plant at Burbank, illustrates the dilemma that faced the whole aviation industry, as well as the military technical agencies. He was somewhat reluctant to accept a fairly large production order because, as he puts it, the company's capitalization was so small. A very small loss on the sales involved might exceed the company's whole capital value. It was paradoxical to contemplate a loss of business-threatening bankruptcy simply by multiplying small units losses by unprecedented numbers. In any event, establishing the credit to approach a job of this magnitude was a problem. Further, the scope of the work involved management and costs beyond the company's experience, raising the possibility of serious error in estimates. The other side of the coin was that a similarly small *profit* on sales would be so overwhelming in terms of return on capital that some congressional investigation would almost surely follow. A reasonably acceptable return on equity capital would have been so insignificant compared to the larger commitment that it would have been impossible to build operating reserves or to plow back money into the plant for operating on the new scale.

The final size of the industrial plant and the organization created to fight the war make a barrier difficult to penetrate in order to appreciate the transition problems. Fortunately, there is one concise record that preserves a review of the situation. The *Aircraft Yearbook of 1948* reprints the texts of the reports from the President's Air Policy Commission of late 1947, the Congressional Aviation Policy Board, and seventeen aircraft companies. The drastic cutbacks in 1945 and 1946 precipitated a crisis that stimulated a review of the previous expansion process and a reevaluation of an adequate defense stature. The statements by the leaders of the various companies are particularly interesting. Many of the facets of the problems are shown, and the whole becomes a guide for mobilization planning.

Although all the reports are revealing, two of the manufacturer's statements are particularly pertinent. Guy W. Vaughan, president of the Curtiss-Wright Corp, stated:

In order to live up to the task assigned us, we were, therefore, required to lay out an expansion program starting from our four plants and ultimately resulting in the operation of 17 plants in 10 localities. Our employment grew from 14,000 in 1940 to 190,000 at the peak of the war. The square footage in our manufacturing plants spread from 1,971,000 at the beginning of 1940 to a total of 24,963,000 square feet in 1944.

Vaughan said that they had to "train over half a million employees," and the impact of this has to be considered. All industry was demanding the same kind of expansion so there were no sources to tap. Each industry had to handle its own problems. If Curtiss had 14,000 employees to start with then, not over half would be in skilled areas that demanded the greatest increases. Trainers had to be trained to train before trainees became available. Even on-the-job training involved distraction of supervisory personnel and less efficient work from the trainees.

James H. Kindelberger, president of North American Aviation, Inc., better known as "Dutch," was well recognized for his concern with production. It used to be said that when a design first took shape, Dutch would personally indicate on the preliminary drawings where the parting lines were to be made, thus determining the basic organization for production, as well as for structural design. In his testimony 15 to the Air Policy Commission, he said:

I have been actively engaged in the airframe manufacturing business for 29 years, the last 13 as president of North American Aviation. The company expanded from 6,000 employees in one plant in the summer of 1940 to some 92,000 in five plants three years later, delivering 13.8 per cent in terms of units and 11.1 per cent in terms of airframe weight of all military airplanes produced by the nation during the war years. Airplanes developed by this company and produced in large volume throughout World War II included the P-51 Mustang fighter, the AT-6 Texan trainer, and the B-25 Mitchell bomber.

THE MANPOWER SITUATION

At the time of the expansion accompanying our entry in the war, a whole decade had passed since the start of the Depression with its ensuing impact on all industry. This resulted in a draining of the pool of skilled and technically trained manpower. Public make-work programs had taken up the slack in many of the unskilled areas, and this in turn had provided supervisory and management positions. However, there were few job openings for engineers, and outputs from colleges were small. Correspondingly, there was a dearth of apprentice training in the highly skilled trades, such as machinist work, which adversely affected the more technical industries such as tool manufacturing.

The demands for manpower in uniform could be partially met by readjustments in the large number of people being supported directly or indirectly by public works. There were many cultural projects supported during the period that did little to provide technical or military manpower. However, the upper layer of administration and supervision did provide a pool having general application, so that even here the indirect benefits were real but limited.

In the technical and production fields, training had to be done by the people who had been doing the work. So the first impact was a loss of skilled effort and an increase in overhead costs. This tended to compound the problem of estimating time and costs for both the procuring agencies and the manufacturers.

In the aircraft industry, a marked change took place when an extra level of engineering with the attendant administrative and cost problems was organized. It resulted from the need for multiplying the output of drawings and detail designs by factors of ten or more. Previously during the 1930s, the chief engineers or project engineers had worked directly with subordinate engineers and experienced draftsmen. These men not only drew the plans but also were fully qualified to do the detailed design involving structural details and production procedures. They worked directly from sketches or principal design layouts. The draftsmen became engineers, which in reality they always had been, and a new level was trained quickly, simply to do the drawing of the detailed manufacturing plans. There were, of course, variations from company to company, but the basic alteration lengthened lines of communication, involved additional levels of review, and added costs and time.

Before World War II, the military services maintained emergency war planning activities. For manpower, these plans included the Reserve and National Guard cadres. For the related industrial planning, there were plans for meeting anticipated requirements for specific weapons and supplies. All such plans had to be based on certain assumptions about the nature of any future emergency and the matériel expected to be in existence. Since these requirements changed continually, the planning process had to be continual, as well. Actual emergencies almost inevitably involve a different set of circumstances than anticipated. However, many different

Rugged and reliable, the North American B-25 Mitchell medium bomber provided valuable tactical support on every major front during World War II while in service with the air forces of the United States and the other Allies.

versions of emergency plans permit the initial mobilization orders to take effect and the planners to be in place with their planning factors and their processes that can be adapted to new situations. Even so, with our stature, our military doctrine, and our political outlook just prior to World War II, we were so unprepared for the nature and magnitude of the emergency as it arose that previous planning was inadequate and improvisation became the guiding force for some time.

While serving as a military observer attached to the American embassy in London during part of 1940, I was told of a critical error in the English planning for emergency. The English Guards regiments were the first line and were of superb quality. As the backup for mobilization, there were reserve units manned and trained but not placed on active duty. With the first rush to mobilize, it was found that the active and patriotic individuals who composed these reserve units were also equally active and competent in their civilian professions. Calling them up left many organizations and activities short of capabilities that were as essential to the overall mobilization effort as manning the combat troop units was. These key people had to be relieved, thus disrupting the manning and deployment of combat units.

The same problem faced the United States in somewhat different form. Deferments of certain key skills from draft requirements was a major consideration during the entire war. In some cases—in the National Advisory Committee for Aeronautics (NACA), for instance—key people were accepted into the services, commissioned as officers, then reassigned to their former activities. In other cases, individuals with special civilian skills were commissioned, then assigned to duties in military organizations corresponding to their civilian specialities.

INDUSTRIAL PLANNING

In the industrial planning area, there were other modifying factors. As weapons developed, there was a need for continual reallocation of facilities and reappraisal of   17

Boeing FB-5s await final assembly in the Boeing plant at Seattle, Washington.

the capability and capacity of sources of supply. Since the scope of the final mobilization could never be accurately stated before the emergency, the potential bottlenecks were obscured. Before the emergency, the then-existing industrial plant of the nation had to be the basis for the allocation of production responsibilities. Although a number of strategic scenarios could be tested, the final allocation of priorities became a top-level political as well as strategic matter. Some of the shifts involved the needs of Navy versus Army versus Air, or shipping versus tanks, airplanes versus cannons. An added factor was the desirable, possible, and probable use of the different forces and their deployment priority.

Some surprises surfaced. Products made in machine shops seemed to be figured most easily. So many machine tools, operated by so many machinists, working so many shifts could obviously produce a predictable output as multiples of the current output of similar machines, operators, and labor hours. Assembly processes were, on the other hand, gross estimates depending upon the skill levels of the workers, the availability of components, the organization of assembly lines, the ingenuity of designers of jigs and fixtures, and floor space. The paradox was that the very flexible nature of the assembly process lent itself to equally flexible solutions. For

Lockheed P-38 Lightnings were assembled in Burbank, California.

instance, when floor space ran out, a lot of assembly work in California was done outdoors. The assembly process never did become the bottleneck that was expected, but the machine process for engines, propellers, landing gears, and similar elements turned out to be the critical pacing factor.

For instance, aircraft were completed and flown to parking areas where propellers were removed and transported back to the factory so that more planes could be pulled out of the assembly areas. At one stage, all the landing gears for P-38s stocked as spares in Air Corps depots were gathered and flown back to the Lockheed factory in order to permit clearing the assembly lines in the factory. As a further step, modification centers were set up to install late arriving equipment and armament and to make changes that could not be accomplished in the regular assembly.

The machine tool industry was a prime example of the situation where "something else had to be done first." Both general and special machine tools had to be built and delivered to the aircraft plants before their capacity could be brought to bear on the end-product weapons. But the expanded demand meant first expanding the capacity of the specialty machine shops that made the machine tools. So the specialty shops had to get more tools and machinists to make the tools, and all 19 segments of industry were demanding the same things. Kindelberger notes that this area was a bottleneck and also points out that the impact rippled all the way back to the sources of raw materials.

The P-38 landing gear situation raises the question of spares manufacture and availability. A procurement policy called "concurrent spares" had evolved during the 1930s. This meant that a certain percentage of production was directed toward the building of spare components simultaneously with the production of flying articles. When only limited numbers of aircraft were available, airplanes grounded for lack of parts critically reduced an already meager force. But with the urgent need for planes to equip the combat units as they were being formed and trained, a temporary measure was adopted to divert the spares production capacity to the making of complete planes.

The more rapid delivery of planes to units without the support of available spares led to cannibalization of out-of-service planes to keep the others flying. This was generally resisted or at least deplored by the technical and procurement agencies because the brunt of the displeasure and criticism from the operating units fell on their shoulders.

At one point, Gen. Henry H. Arnold called a meeting of key officers from the Matériel Division to establish the urgency of new priorities. With about thirty officers present, he started by saying, "Since you won't give me the spares . . . ." He was interrupted by a resounding "Who won't give who spares, General?" Insubordination? No, he had just touched a sensitive nerve. He immediately changed the subject to self-sealing tanks and heavier armament. It had never been contemplated that the spare parts pool or the spares production capacity would become a "surge tank" or reservoir for increasing complete airplane fabrication, but the policy change, although temporary, was one of the unpleasant expedients that had to be taken at the time.

PRODUCTION ESTIMATES

At the time when the probability of the need for expansion of the services first became urgent, President Franklin Roosevelt "requested" a report from Wright Field indicating the maximum production capability of the aircraft industry. Like all such "requests," the time allowed for submittal was too short to permit a complete or comprehensive study. Using the industrial emergency plans and with the extensive cooperation of the industry, estimates were put together. At the time, the results seemed unduly optimistic, but they later turned out to be quite accurate.

One of the ground rules, stated or implied, was that this estimate was to be based on the existing capital plant without the secondary impact of possible expansion. Curtiss, as an example, indicated that its production of P-40s could be increased from one plane a day to ten. It was pointed out that at the higher rate it would be only a very short time before the supply on hand of raw materials and purchased parts would be exhausted. This revealed two important factors. One was that the industry had been working at a pace artificially restrained by production funding. This meant that the plant, if used to capacity and manned by three shifts, each day, would have a vastly increased capability. The other factor that surfaced was that, to be meaningful, the second-order problems required thorough investigation by going back in the production cycle all the way to the basics, such as aluminum production.

At Wright Field, aware of the deficiencies in these first estimates, it was hoped that the initial orders for increased production would adhere to a ground rule of no capital plant expansion. This would have developed the bottlenecks in second- and third-order items. The shortcomings in basic production of raw materials, forgings,

By World War II, specialized tooling greatly reduced the number of man-hours required to fabricate sheet metal parts.

and machining might have been revealed. As it happened, time did not permit the more orderly approach, and the first expansions were uneven, resulting in critical delays and shortages in unexpected categories.

Estimating the industrial base from which these expansions took place is difficult. Many small companies and individual builders would not have been rated as potential sources. The aircraft that they built were generally light commercial or special-purpose types. With mobilization, some of the outfits made substantial contributions in trainers, small transports, and components for combat types. Cessna, Beech, Stearman, Ryan, and Fairchild were among those responding in a significant way. In addition, even the small production levels of the 1930s supported the manufacture of parts and engines, and provided trained personnel as a nucleus for expansion.

It is equally difficult, and probably futile, to try to establish a prewar total production base. It would vary so widely with the selection of date and categories of types as to be meaningless. To grasp the impact of the magnitude of the change, it is probably enough to realize that the president's announced goal, in 1940, of 50,000 military planes a year was perhaps a hundred times the output of these types a few years earlier. It is surprising that the goal was approximately reached in 1942, and by

1944 it was exceeded by 100 percent.

Some easement into the problems of increasing output was provided by foreign sales to England and France. For instance, Pratt & Whitney still, in 1979, called one of the units in its plant the French Building and another the English Building. They were built to furnish engines to these countries because the company's otherwise limited facilities were taxed by our own requirements. Astute negotiating that anticipated our forthcoming military needs enabled these capital plant expansions to be financed by surcharges on the engines delivered.

The problems of production expansion, known as "the numbers racket," are in retrospect, more or less self-evident. The term *racket* came from the serious questions involving numbers versus quality or performance. Both aspects of the problem stemmed from the insignificant base from which the buildup had to start. This was the result of meager support for procurement and development for the preceding 20 years. More subtle and more difficult was the problem of maintaining technical progress and having available the modern types of aircraft suitable for committing to production. Since the lead time from inception to the appearance of a type in appreciable quantity in the service varied from three to seven years, it is evident that most of what appeared in the war had to have been initiated in the mid-1930s.

From the late 1920s to the 1930s, aeronautical technology was changing rapidly and drastically. Materials, construction, aerodynamics, performance, complexity, and power-plant changes took place in a short time. Even if the service force had been modern at any one time, it would have become obsolescent in three or four

That woodworking was labor intensive is evident in this view of wing panels being constructed on a jig.

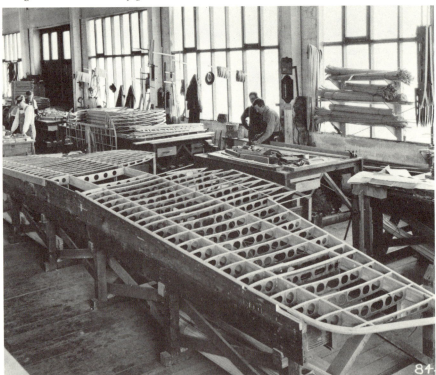

years. To have maintained a combat-ready force would have dictated complete replacement at about this rate. Such a rate was never even contemplated.

Added to obsolescence was the natural loss from old age and accident. Since there had been little attempt to increase the force to an operational level, the production rate for the 20 years before expansion had failed to meet attrition and obsolescence requirements. The result was that a large proportion of the force in existence was made up of older planes with inferior performances. This had started with the continued use of World War I types during the 1920s, which kept pushing into the future the replacement programs that would have stimulated modernization. Only the oldest and least potent articles were pushed out of the bottom of the inventory without changing significantly the proportion of types representing combat capability.

It is little wonder that boards and commissions investigating defense posture consistently found deficiencies. The total numbers in inventory included trainers and utility types as well. These totals were used for political evaluations and budget purposes. The numerous investigative reports varied in emphasis and frames of reference but tended to be consistent in determining that between one-third and one-half of the inventory was not worth counting in a recapitulation of combat readiness.

Planning for replacements involves, first, the improvement of existing types of aircraft. In some respects, this gives rise to the oft-quoted criticism of planning for the last war. But the character of the next war is unknown, and the current missions and functions can be projected into a variety of new possibilities. So it was to be

By the mid-1930s, the construction of all-metal wings on aircraft had become common.

expected that development continued for some plane types that failed to find use in World War II. For instance, the medium-sized observation types, typically 0-47 and 0-52, were improved right up to 1940. The light attack types, similar to the German Stukas, were only slowly replaced by multi-engine light bombers. Scarce engineering skills and production capacity had to be used to protect these capabilities, but at least a *small* potential capability was kept active. Some of the more advanced ideas could not have received support.

The double-barreled problem of maintaining a potential source of modern equip-

Using features from two of its other airplanes (Hawk III retractable landing gear and the SO3C Seagull's collapsible rear turtledeck), Curtiss built 203 0-52s to serve as trainers in World War II.

ment while sustaining a "reorder capability" was difficult and continuing. The ideal was to have a plane of each basic type, such as fighters or bombers, in some stage of production to permit continuing or expanding production in an emergency. With the gaps in procurement of the different basic types, this was impossible. Considerable use had to be made of the permissive and flexible portions of the 1926 federal act H.R. 10827. This was titled the Army Five-Year Aviation Program, but it included a fundamental provision for procurement methods to be used by both the Army and the Navy.

DIFFERING VIEWPOINTS

Coupled with the difficulties inherent in developing new aircraft types that incorporate evolving technology was the problem of reconciling the views of the politicians, the Navy, and the Army. It must be recalled that the results of World War I, while providing convincing evidence for those who foresaw a future for aviation, left almost everyone else in doubt about the value of military aircraft or even their proper function. The previous combat demonstration was elementary, and a reasonable conclusion was that aviation had in no material way influenced the outcome. The benefits of creating a major air arm, or independent force, had to be taken on faith.

The airmen and a few others had no doubts and were not backward in pressing their case. Not a little of the problem was based in the hope that proof of adequacy would never again arise in serious proportions. There were very real reservations *whether*, as well as what and how much, aviation was needed.

The compromises and decisions that were reached in the 1930s have been construed generally to have restricted aviation unduly. There is no doubt that aviation was depressed, but it cannot be assumed that other elements were thereby improperly benefited. There just was not enough of anything to go around. From the vantage point of time, the compromises were "elegant" and "nice," if precise definitions of these terms are used.

There were also difficulties arising within each service and even within the air branches of each service. The Navy's first recognition of the scouting value of aircraft led to the development of scout planes on floats launched from capital ships and recovered alongside from the water. Then as carriers came into being, the bombing and torpedo-carrying types of aircraft evolved, with striking power in their own right. Now, there was a conflict over the *proper* role of air. Then, fighters became necessary for the defense of the floating striking force. During these transitions, the airmen were urging more active participation and a larger portion of financial support for the air arm. Although integration was easier in the Navy than in the Army as far as control, supply, and training were concerned, there were difficult reconciliations between the traditional concepts and the newly developing ones.

This all too simple outline presumes an orderly progression and neglects many facets. Float planes were in continuous use throughout the war, and the growing importance of carriers did not eliminate the scouting and observation function for the surface ships. Also passed over lightly was the role of the Marines. Their mission required land-based planes similar to the Army's for close support of ground operations. The Navy was the development and procurement agency for the Marine Corps. Not only were fighter types needed for the Navy, but the Marines always had active fighter forces. During the late 1920s and early 1930s, Navy and Air Corps fighter types were the same basic aircraft from the same sources with special provisions in the Navy versions for arresting gear, attachment of floats, flotation, and so forth. By the late 1930s, the Navy sources such as Vought and Grumman became more specialized. As the Navy became stronger in the air and the threat of an independent Air Force waned, the conflict between the air arms of the Army and Navy tended to die out. But the question of "roles and missions" between Army and Navy remained pertinent right up to the early days of the war.

Receiving more public attention was the thrust of the Air Corps for larger planes and greater independence from the control of Army command. Inside the Air Corps, a less noticeable but nevertheless difficult division occurred. The big-bomber contingent envisioned bomber forces providing their own fire power and operating at ranges beyond the capabilities of fighters. The only remaining fighter function then would be the protection of bases and friendly ground forces. Fighters consequently suffered from low priority.

Another factor was introduced by advancing technology. Few envisaged the vastly increased load-carrying capability of the relatively small planes or the evolution of the heavily loaded fighter-bomber. In fact, carrying external loads was prohibited on fighters right up to the beginning of hostilities.

To understand the persistence of what seemed to be outmoded concepts and the vehemence of the air protagonists, it is necessary to appreciate the fundamental interrelationship of political and military responsibilities. The essence of military reponsibility is that it must provide a reasonable guarantee of ability to support the political determinations of the nation, whether they be solely defensive security or the protection of some other vital interests.

Each segment of the military then justifiably assumes a need for unlimited call upon the nation's resources. The claims must be stated; they cannot be curtailed before all of them are weighed against each other and a compromise reached. There may be "limited war" in an offensive sense, but there cannot be a *planned* "limited defense," for this is not defense at all.

During the period of change and growth before World War II, all the diverse interests continued to express their views and fight for the satisfaction of each particular facet of the larger problem. This essentially democratic process caused friction, and there were career casualties. But what really mattered was that the varying and conflicting positions were out in the open for evaluation and compromise.

In summary, it was possible to shorten time somewhat in the preamble to expansion by taking advantage of the needs of the English and French. Skillful negotiation by a few key people who anticipated our coming needs provided an initial momentum. Even this small increment, compared to the requirements of the next few years, posed difficult problems. But the real challenges took place five to ten years earlier when the technology, management, and development were established. Aviation, throughout its relatively short history, has been outstanding for its rapid evolution, but the atmosphere of the ten to fifteen years before 1940 put a terrible strain on progress. The slender thread maintained in an apathetic and almost hostile atmosphere made the accomplishments of the war years seem all the more remarkable.

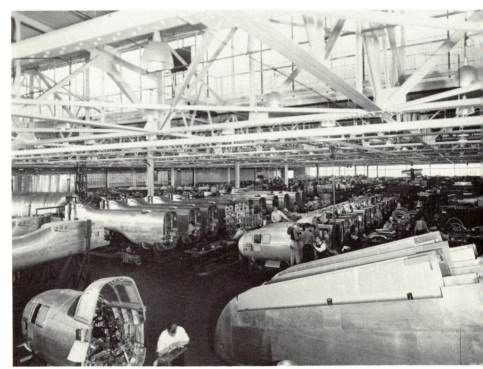

Built in Baltimore, Maryland, the Martin Maryland bomber was delivered in 1940 to the Royal Air Force, which used it primarily on reconnaissance missions.

26

II THE ATMOSPHERE OF THE 1930s

A few days after Charles A. Lindbergh's transatlantic flight, the price of the stock of the Seaboard Airline rose sharply on the New York Stock Exchange. The Seaboard "Airline" was actually the East Coast *railway* serving the route between New York and Florida. Neither the investment community nor the company was aware of any situation in the company itself that would justify the increase in value, but the public, caught up in the enthusiam over the "Lone Eagle" and his accomplishment, figured that anything associated with aviation, even if in name only, now had a future.

If the buying spree was in fact triggered by the name "Airline," it reveals a few factors associated with the mood of the time, including a suddenly aroused awareness of the potential value of flight in all its aspects. At certain precise moments in history, there is often a marked change in the rate of progress for almost every activity. May 21, 1927, was definitely one of those points for aviation.

Previous transatlantic flights, flights of geographical exploration, record flights for speed and distance, the establishment of commercial air mail routes should have made the public aware of the emerging significance of air travel. But these events had apparently been taken as remote and unconnected incidents. Undoubtedly, there was a growing, but latent, recognition of the significance of flight in commerce and in military operations that needed only the drama of the Lindbergh flight to tip the scales beyond the critical point.

A NEW EPOCH

Soon after the Lindbergh flight, many people not previously connected with aviation—lawyers, financiers, promoter types, salesmen, engineers, and manufacturers—looked for opportunities in the burgeoning field. Aviation innovators, pilots, and small-scale constructors found it easier to organize and finance aviation enterprises.

Previously, "barnstormers," living like gypsies and flying World War I surplus airplanes, declared that they were selling aviation to the public. Undoubtedly they did, in a way, but carrying one or two passengers at a time for thrills, putting on acrobatic shows, taking occasional aerial photographs, and now and then carrying an enthusiast on a cross-country business trip made discouragingly slow headway. It was rather like tilling a large field with a hand hoe and about as productive.

Even these pioneers suddenly became businessmen, swapping their nomadic existences for operations from newly created "airports." They became known as fixed-base operators and created a demand for new planes with improved performance and reliability. This demand filtered back to the builders who then incorporated new structural concepts that replaced the "stick and wire" fuselages and wings of the previous war. New engines with improved reliability and more efficient perform- 27 ance began to appear.

The recurring debates over the relative merits of wood versus metal construction had abated. It is now difficult to appreciate the intensity of the contentions that wood was the *only* suitable material for aircraft construction. Although liquid-cooled in-line or V engines had become almost standard during the course of the war with the disappearance of the air-cooled rotary, air-cooled radial engines in the smaller sizes had almost taken over from the war-surplus types. The Wright 220-h.p. Whirlwind, which Lindbergh had used, was more powerful than most of the engines in general use. The 400-h.p. Liberty, the United States's liquid-cooled V engine produced in large quantities, continued in use for some time, and there were newer liquid-cooled V types of equal and higher power developed for military applications. But even in the higher powers, the air-cooled radials by Wright and Pratt & Whitney were becoming available for military and commercial transport operations.

The emergence of higher powered air-cooled engines in the 400- to 500-h.p. class raised the question of the relative merits of liquid versus air cooling, a question that had a serious impact on all decisions affecting military aircraft procurement and development right up to World War II. Although particularly applicable to the small, higher performance fighters—or "pursuit" as they were designated then—the basic considerations were never really settled until the jet and turbine engines eliminated the issue.

The air-cooled engines simplified installations and eliminated the vulnerability of the liquid-cooled systems to battle damage. They also reduced problems with spares and logistics and perhaps added some measure of reliability. On the other hand, where maximum performance was paramount, the liquid-cooled engines offered smaller frontal areas and corresponding reductions in drag because of the easier refinement of their external contours. There was also some benefit with the liquid-

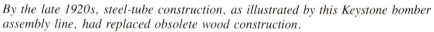

By the late 1920s, steel-tube construction, as illustrated by this Keystone bomber assembly line, had replaced obsolete wood construction.

cooled system in being able to locate the cooling radiators in the most advantageous position for drag and balance.

This issue was more than a simple question of technical selection of the most suitable equipment for a given mission. It was a highly charged political issue in the sense that major questions of policy and support were involved. In an era of shortages of almost everything, funding and application of manpower were such serious problems that multiple approaches were automatically suspect.

One of the major development and production efforts in the United States had been the building of the Liberty 12-cylinder, 400-h.p. engine; as many as 10,000 of them remained in inventory in 1925. The Wright Company had been building versions of the Hispano Suiza, a French liquid-cooled 8-cylinder V engine, rated from 150 to 300 h.p. This latter engine powered the Thomas Morse MB-3. Fifty-four of these planes were built by Thomas Morse, with 200 more made by Boeing—the largest order for any single type of plane until 1939 and the P-40s. Most of the other immediate postwar military types used the Liberty or modifications of it. One of the modifications was an inverted version built by the Allison Company, a small machine shop in Indianapolis near the Speedway. Allison's bread-and-butter business was a proprietary bearing that was used in their rebuilding of Liberties and in other applications.

A number of engines, some of high power, were under development right after the war. These dropped out of the picture except for the Curtiss D-12 of 400 h.p. for service use and 500 and 600 h.p. in racing versions, the Wright Tornado of 600 h.p., and the Packard 1A-1500 of 600 h.p. and the 1A-2500 of 800 h.p. The only one of these having reasonably extensive service use was the D-12 and its derivatives up to the Conquerer, built by Wright after the Curtiss-Wright merger. Although installations in new aircraft stopped in 1933, many continued in use for several more years.

The Boeing PW-9 was powered by a 435-h.p. Curtiss D-12 engine and had a top speed of 155 mph.

ENGINE DEVELOPMENT

Liquid-cooled engines stayed in use for a number of years in the Air Corps, but the Navy early in the 1920s established the policy that engines for shipboard planes should be air-cooled. This was both logical and natural for the Navy. Since all spares and supplies had to be carried when leaving port, the elimination of cooling system parts and coolant was a matter of considerable importance. There was some gain in reliability, which had a considerable psychological effect during long over-water flights. There had been some Navy types procured during the early 1920s with Liberty, D-12, and Packard engines, but by 1927 or 1928 air-cooled installations were standard.

Commercial operators, for reasons similar to the Navy's, universally adopted the air-cooled solution. Here, there was an advantage in simpler maintenance. Since commercial and export production practically sustained the industry in times of restricted military procurement, the air-cooled engines were more intensively developed and appeared in more models.

What seems now to have been purely a technical problem for settling in the engineering departments actually was more involved. Adding to the confusion was the admirable work of the NACA from about 1926 to 1928 in developing cowling for the air-cooled engines that improved drag and cooling. For airplanes in the 200-mph bracket, speed capabilities were improved by 20 mph. The information was widely disseminated, and the designs equally widely accepted. For this work, the NACA deservedly received the 1930 Collier Trophy, the National Aeronautic Association's annual award for greatest achievement in aeronautics.

Now that most of the performance objections to air cooling had been eliminated, the reason for liquid cooling seemed to disappear. The Navy, or "first line of defense," having established a policy of using air-cooled engines, satisfied the primary requirement for the military; the commercial and export markets, having assumed the same preference, justified the support of air-cooled development and supported quantity production.

Since the United States had just barely recovered from the "war to end all war" and was in an emotional atmosphere of "peace at any price," it was natural that a development that seemed applicable only to the Army Air Corps, and even to a limited part of it at best, attracted considerable opposition. This controversial, sometimes hostile, attitude persisted from the mid-1920s through the Depression, through Adolf Hitler's *Mein Kampf* and German rearmament, right up to the threshold of World War II. So by about 1933, the air-cooled engines were substantially dominant in both military and commercial aircraft.

But there were plenty of indications that for maximum performance the potential of liquid-cooled engines should not be overlooked. In the early 1920s, American planes and pilots were setting world's speed records with the big V-12 liquid-cooled engines. As support for these record attempts in this country was withdrawn, the records went to Europe, first to the British and then to the Italians. Starting a few years before, the Air Corps had by 1929 or 1930 standardized the use of ethylene glycol for high-temperature cooling. This higher temperature permitted cutting the size of radiators in half. The resulting gain in streamlining and in cooling drag just about matched the air-cooled improvements obtained with the NACA cowling. The net effect was that the *potential* margin of difference remained, but at a higher efficiency level. Later on in the late 1930s, the British, using some of the technology developed for the Supermarine racers and Rolls-Royce engines, built fighters that seemed to have higher performances than the corresponding American types. Then, the Germans with the Messerschmitt 209 special racer set a new speed record in

Winner of the 1931 Schneider Trophy Cup, the Supermarine S6B developed into the Supermarine Spitfire.

1939 of 469 mph or, as was reported in the 1940 *Janes All The World Aircraft*, 481 mph. These were all with liquid-cooled engines. By comparison with the liquid-cooled development abroad, the American efforts were almost insignificant.

By the mid-1930s, the evolutionary development of producing liquid-cooled engines had petered out with the last installations of the Curtiss-Wright Conqueror in the Air Corps PB-2As. New developments aimed at much higher powers, starting at 1,000 h.p. were started about 1930, based on the higher temperature cooling of ethylene glycol. Both the Navy and Army supported these developments but at a level that meant very slow progress. As was the case with other development funding by the services throughout this period, government funding probably covered less than half the actual costs. Certainly if it had not been for the substantial investment by General Motors, which had acquired Allison in 1929, the Allison V-1710 would not have become available in 1936 as a 1,000-h.p. engine.

In the late 1930s, the Air Corps, in an effort to boost performance, reinstituted liquid-cooled applications in a number of experimental planes, XFM-1, XP-37, XP-38, XP-39, XP-40. With the 1939 procurement of P-40s, service use was started. During the whole period, the engine development agencies of the services were concerned with any potential power plant development that promised increased power.

AIR POWER

Among the factors that influenced most of the decisions and actions in the creation of air power during the 1930s were many matters like the liquid cooling issue, within 31

The Bell YP-39 was a major disappointment as an interceptor despite its radical mid-engine approach.

the services and the rest of the federal government. Government procurement regulations and their interpretation, desires for a separate air force, the concept of naval air doctrine, and the differences between the Navy and the Army in the integration of aviation also had a profound affect.

One of the best explanations of "air power" is contained in the record of the hearings before the President's Aircraft Board of 1925. It includes the fundamental interaction of *external* public and political factors with the *internal* industrial and military considerations. Howard E. Coffin, a board member, said that one of the several elements is "a definite, comprehensive, and continuing Federal policy for the furtherance of aeronautical progress in all its various phases, based on a 10 year appropriation and development program."

Following the 1925 action of the President's Board, or the Morrow Board as it was known because Dwight Morrow had been the chairman, Congress in 1926 set the stage for a new era. It passed the Army Five Year Aviation Program, the Navy Five Year Aviation Program, and a Civil Aeronautics Act. With this basis, it remained for the Lindbergh flight to stir the public and political appreciation of air power that the first parts of the Coffin definition indicated were necessary.

The Army program did much more than authorize increases in planes and personnel. It established the *Air Corps* thereby giving more stature to Army aviation, though this action remained considerably short of the desires of the more enthusiastic advocates of a separate air force. It provided for temporary grades and for the selection of chiefs of corps and assistant chiefs, if they had as much as fifteen years service, to hold suitable temporary rank. The programs for both services did much to rectify disparities in grade and responsibility within the air arms.

In computing the number of serviceable planes for budgeting purposes, the programs acknowledged the factor of obsolescence by providing for the replacement of not more than 400 planes per year in the Air Corps and of something over 300 aircraft varying from year to year for the Navy. The Army program authorized an increase in Air Corps personnel from about 900 men in 1925 to 1,500 officers within five years. This level, however, was far short of the 4,000 that the Lassiter Committee (appointed in 1923 by Secretary of War John W. Weeks to study the Air

Corp's needs) had said was necessary to maintain an adequate force.

The authorized increases in aircraft for the Air Corps to 1,800 was far short of desired levels, and the increase was scheduled to take place over five years. This number seems to have roughly corresponded to the reported strengths of foreign air forces. Since the current strength at the time was about 1,100 planes of all sorts, of which 300 to 400 were considered first line, it was a start. Actually, there never had been *any* chance of funding the *desired* levels. In fact, the situation in the Air Corps continued to worsen until about 1935.

PROCUREMENT PROCEDURES

Most significant in the 1926 act was the detailed definition of competitive procurement procedures, which remained in force with some interpretative modifications all through the 1930s until the War Powers Act. These provisions applied to both the Army and the Navy.

Prior to the Air Commerce Act of 1926, the only regulation of civil air activity had been by some states. These regulations lacked uniformity, and of course air traffic was insensitive to state boundaries. The provisions of the federal act were the basis for the implementation in 1927 of licensing, inspection, and regulation.

As Coffin and the board so aptly foresaw, the Lindbergh flight touched the man in the street. He could now take pride in an American aeronautical achievement that had attracted worldwide acclaim. He could identify with the accomplishment of one man. He could easily see the possibilities of long-range flight for himself and his goods. Perhaps subconsciously, he appreciated that military aviation could be something more than a "dogfight" over some remote foreign battlefield.

There had already been some early civil air operations that indicated potential developments other than the flying school and local passenger carrying operations. Sherman Fairchild had parlayed a surplus World War I aerial camera into an aerial photographic business. Huff-Daland had built twenty crop-dusting planes and, borrowing Harold Harris (an Air Service lieutenant, head of flight testing at

The Curtiss JN-4, "Jenny," was the standard training plane of the First World War. Thousands were used after the war to carry the mail and "barnstorm" around the country.

33

McCook Field) from the Army, had been running an economically solid agricultural operation since 1925. The air mail operations pioneered by the Post Office Department had been transferred to commercial operators, and the service was growing. One more factor helped to set the stage. This time period coincided with the significant decline in availability of war surplus equipment.

The problems had been recognized, and guidelines for correction had been established even though correction itself was a long way off. The public was intrigued, and politicians could safely support aviation projects. By 1928, even the prospects for engineers seemed bright. Thanks to the far-sighted and generous support of the Guggenheim Foundation for the Advancement of Aviation, schools such as MIT, New York University, and Cal Tech had expanded their aeronautical engineering schools. Their graduates were now in demand.

The established manufacturers such as Boeing, Curtiss, Douglas, Vought, and Martin had highly competent and dedicated engineering staffs. The engine companies, including Pratt & Whitney and Wright, were well staffed for the scale of their business. The NACA laboratories were expanding their facilities and were supplying a wealth of basic material of widely recognized significance and value. In addition, the military services maintained technical schools and engaged in active research programs. In all cases, the number of people and the funding were small. There was, however, the prospect of expansion.

Springing up throughout the country were a large number of small operators and aviation-related activities that needed staffs to match the growing demands. Previously, some of these had been almost one-man operations where the pioneer had been engineer, production manager, financier, and salesman all in one. Some of these outfits survived, for a time at least, and made significant contributions.

The new airlines in addition to their operating staffs were beginning to acquire engineering people to work on specifications, maintenance, and operational performance. All in all, the aircraft industry, and to a lesser extent military aviation, was acquiring status and stature.

But then the Depression of 1929 killed the easy credit and the enthusiasm of the last couple of years. It is difficult to appraise the magnitude of the impact on aviation as a whole during the next six or seven years. In some respects, it is evident that only the fittest survived. This may have weeded out a lot of fly-by-night operations and grandiose plans, but it carried away many worthwhile activities and killed the momentum that had just begun to build.

The preoccupation with personal and national economic survival relegated avia-

Many war surplus de Havilland D.H.4 bombers were used by the Post Office to carry the mail. Several were modified with different wings and other equipment.

tion and military affairs to very low priority in the political and public consciousness. The psychological impact lasted beyond the pure economic impact and influenced military aviation unfavorably right up to entry into World War II. Because of the close interconnection of military and civil concerns in aviation activity as a whole, aviation probably was depressed further and longer than any other industrial or technical component of our society.

COMMERCIAL AVIATION

In a modest way, one segment of the aeronautical community was on an expanding cycle and continued to make steady progress. The airlines, principally because of airmail contracts or subsidies, were able to extend their operations and purchase newer types of planes. The required transport types generally represented larger, more sophisticated, and higher performance aircraft. Their production involved newer technology, competent engineering, development of production techniques, appropriate total metal structures, extensive testing, and full consideration of safety and reliability.

Although the numbers of aircraft in the transport category remained small, their design and construction provided a sound and persistent thread of technology that applied to all air operations. This factor was the principal means of keeping our aircraft competitive with foreign developments and permitted transfer of the technology to military types as the need arose.

Transition periods, which in retrospect seem unnecessary, did occur. One of these is represented by the Boeing 40B, a single-engine biplane. This plane included a small, four-passenger cabin in front of the pilot, who flew from an open cockpit well aft. While the plane was primarily a mail plane, it sought to induce some daring souls to accompany the mail on scheduled flights. As a passenger transport, it seems incongruous today, but it has to be recognized that a hackneyed phrase was still commonly heard, "I'll take a flight if I can keep one foot on the ground." It was only a few years since the barnstormers had used the gimmick of a shoe box full of dirt on the cockpit floor for the reluctant prospective passenger to put his foot in while taking a flight.

When the commercial airmail contracts replaced the government airmail service, the modified D.H.4s that had been used were phased out. Then came relatively small single-engine commercial biplanes, such as Pitcairn Mailwings, Curtiss Larks, and Douglas M-2s, which were simply more modern versions of the D.H.s.

The Boeing 40B was the first aircraft designed to carry passengers as well as mail.

But the Boeing 40 B represented the conceptual beginning of combined passenger and cargo flight.

There were some routes that used small cabin monoplanes; one was route No. 1, Boston–New York, which started with Fokker Universals. On the West Coast, there were Ryans, Northrops, and Lockheeds, which were similar small, single-engine monoplanes. These were all primarily passenger planes carrying mail. The construction of these planes served primarily to keep a few struggling companies alive.

The concept of long-range, over-water flight was a natural development from the extensive use of the large patrol flying boats by the Allied navies during World War I. The transatlantic flight of the NC-4 was the forerunner of the transoceanic routes flown with large flying boats up to World War II. As early as 1920, there were conversions of large boats such as the wartime F-5L into passenger transports. From the pioneering efforts of airlines including New York, Rio, and Buenos Aires and Pan Am came the demand for new, better, and larger flying boats. Sikorsky, Consolidated, Martin, and later Boeing carried the development into the large four-engined Clippers.

Over land, there were additional transitional developments. Night flying had been conducted even with the D.H.s of the Air Mail Service. Passenger traffic justified Ford and Fokker trimotors for the growing commercial airline business, but night flying facilities were inadequate for this scale of operation. Slow average flying speeds, probably less than 100 mph, made transcontinental flights take almost a full 24-hour day. Ground facilities were marginal to nonexistent for handling night passenger travel safely and conveniently. Consequently, a number of arrangements were made with railroads to combine air and rail service.

Transcontinental Air Transport, one of the components of what was later TWA,

Combining the general design of the Fokker F.VII/3m with the corrugated, all-metal construction pioneered by Junkers, the Ford Tri-motor became the mainstay of American commercial transports in the late 1920s and early 1930s.

worked out a plan with the Pennsylvania and Santa Fe railroads to provide transcontinental service. A luxury service started in July, 1929, departing from New York in the afternoon by rail overnight to Columbus, Ohio. From the railroad siding at the airport, the passengers boarded TAT Ford Trimotors for a flight to Waynoka, Oklahoma. After dinner, they boarded the Santa Fe Pullmans for an overnight rail trip to Clovis, New Mexico. After breakfast, they again took to the air for a flight to Los Angeles. What with enroute refueling stops and time for ground travel and meals, the elapsed time was 48 hours, but the service attracted a great deal of attention.

The combined rail-air service lasted a little over a year and was supplanted by two daylight flight legs with an overnight stop in Kansas City. This shortened the time to 36 hours. However, the need for night-flying facilities stimulated both commercial and governmental investment. Both night and weather flying were conducted, primarily with single-engine mail planes, but the night passenger service was delayed for several years. However, the increasing passenger traffic emphasized the need for larger and faster transports.

A transition step to remove the inconvenience of night flight was the sleeper plane. Since the aircraft had berths like a Pullman car, it was possible for a few passengers to enjoy the luxury of going to bed while traveling. The ones who sat up withstood the discomfort to save money. Soon, it became evident that those who felt the urge to fly in order to save time were willing to accept inconvenience, and the sleeper disappeared.

NEW DEVELOPMENTS

With the appearance of the Boeing 247 in 1932, a new trend began. Although the elements of the design configuration had been used previously—cantilever monoplane wing, twin engine, retractable landing gear, all-metal construction, enclosed cockpit and cabin, easy aft entrance for passengers—they were synthesized into an attractive and relatively high performance craft. United Air Lines ordered fifty-nine of them for the transcontinental route from San Francisco to Chicago and New York.

Because Boeing was involved in the contract with United, the other airlines approached Douglas, which used a similar but slightly larger configuration to produce the DC-3. With modifications, this type survived through the war and even had some limited postwar production.

With the increase in regular commercial flight schedules and longer range missions for military operations, weather flying became more important. This led to the development of instrumentation, aviation facilities, and instrument-flying technique. It is interesting to reflect on how often developments originate well back in time but must wait for growing demand to bring them into general use. This had been true of instrument or weather flying.

The older technique of flying in bad weather was to follow railroads, highways, or other landmarks, staying under clouds and out of areas of seriously restricted visibility, landing whenever going on became difficult or impossible. This frequently involved landing in "unprepared" fields—actually pastures, golf courses, and convenient, or often inconvenient, open spaces.

In spite of the recognition as early as 1912 or 1913 that human senses were inadequate to control an airplane without outside visual references, many pilots until quite late thought that it was possible to fly "blind" by feel alone. The possibility of supplementing human senses appeared as early as 1920. A bank-and-turn indicator, a gyro instrument, was displayed at the New York Air Show in the 59th Street Armory. The instrument had been invented two years before by Lawrence Sperry, 37 but it took several more years to come into general use.

A few ardent enthusiasts tried to push the installation and use of these simple instruments. They were not appreciated. One, Maj. William C. Ocker of the Army Air Service, carried a bank-and-turn instrument around as personal property along with a venturi suction unit. He wired, clamped, or taped these to each plane he flew. He irked so many people that he was required to take a psychiatric examination. He claimed afterward that he was the only officer in the service who could prove that he was sane; he had the papers to show it.

In a 1925 issue of *National Geographic* magazine, John A. Macready and Oakley G. Kelly cited the bank-and-turn instrument as an essential factor in the success of their transcontinental flight of 1923. Over the desert at night, where reference points were nonexistent, they had relied on the gyro instrument to maintain their attitude. Some of the airliners, a few individuals in these services, and the instrument companies continued working on the instrument problem; but the work was very low key. There was still little demand for this new capability. The transoceanic flights were isolated instances of instrument flight, and, of course, Lindbergh's flight served to dramatize this aspect as well.

In 1929, the Guggenheim Fund for the Promotion of Aeronautics established a Full Flight Laboratory to develop the means for complete blind flight including takeoffs and landings. James H. Doolittle, then a lieutenant on loan from the Army, was the director and pilot. The support of this effort was yet another of the significant contributions of the Guggenheims to the progress of aviation. With the participation of Sperry, Paul Kollsman, Harry Diamond of the Bureau of Standards, and others, the instruments, navigation equipment and facilities, and necessary flying procedures were developed, so that in a few months it was possible to demonstrate complete blind flights (including takeoffs and landings).

This demonstration was perhaps the most significant development since the original Wright brothers' flight. It made the front page of the *New York Times* for an issue but attracted little public interest. The last paragraph of the final report by Doolittle and the foundation found it advisable to reiterate the need for adequate instrumentation and training in order to fly blind. It was still only marginally recognized.

THE AIRMAIL EPISODE

In February, 1934, all the outstanding airmail contracts were cancelled. This stemmed from allegations by a radio commentator that there had been improprieties in the allocation of routes some years previously. A congressional committee, headed by Alabama Sen. Hugo Black, conducted an investigation and concluded that small operators had been discriminated against and big companies had been favored. By executive order, President Roosevelt cancelled the contracts with the civil operators and directed the Army Air Corps to take over the operation on several of the routes. This action apparently was politically oriented and aimed at discrediting Herbert Hoover's previous administration.

The ensuing operation was plagued by mishaps. All but one of the crashes were in connection with administrative flights, ferrying training, or communications. Nevertheless, the press took advantage of the situation to build up the difficulties and overlook the positive aspects. The fact that older airplanes were kept in service because of the lack of funds for replacement was neglected in comparing performance of the Army planes with the newer commercial transports. The same situation applied to instrument and radio equipment. There was a tendency to cite a lack of proficiency and training on the part of the military pilots. Somehow, these comments seemed to originate in the same quarters that had for years decried the funding of expenses for the military. The result had been to curtail operational training to four hours per month for extended periods, which was not enough to maintain familiarity with the equipment let alone conduct tactical training.

Most of the investigations by committees and boards conducted up to this date had been sympathetic to the aviation industry. The Black committee was obviously critical and did not respect the secondary impact on the industry as a whole. While most of the other reports were only marginal in their impact on the public, this one had profound effects not only on the public and the political atmosphere but also on the future of civil and military aviation. Conclusions drawn at the time were almost universally erroneous. Only a few individuals had recognized by 1940 that the airmail episode had been a key factor in preparing the nation for the war emergency.

The news media had been caught in a perplexing situation. First, it looked as though a scandal might be in the making. Then, the airlines reacted. It had been necessary to provide a "subsidy" in the form of airmail contracts to expand the airline routes and support the buildup to full-fledged passenger, express, and mail service.

Incidentally, Lindbergh released a telegram strongly criticizing President Roosevelt's action. Lindbergh was not a completely unbiased participant, since he worked as a consultant to several of the airlines. He was, however, highly respected and considered entirely honest. This embarrassed the President, who responded critically, and this set up an antagonism that lasted all through World War II. Although subsequent investigations cleared most of the allegations and pretty well established that no illegal actions had taken place, the first reaction was to accept the scandal thesis.

The next step was to be critical of the political elements. This was difficult for the news media because the administration was immensely popular as the symbol of dynamic leadership guiding the way out of the Depression. The Air Corps then became the scapegoat, and Gen. Benjamin D. Foulois, the chief of Air Corps, was severely criticized.

The details of the operation and the subsequent events deserve expansion under the heading of the military and industrial establishment. By the middle of May, the Air Corps activity had started to close down and was ended by June. Temporary contracts were awarded, with some face-saving provisions, and the whole business was pushed into the background.

Paradoxically, for the first time aviation was on the one hand important enough to be a significant political and economic issue while on the other hand it was something that would be attacked without concern for the criticism's effect on national security or economic progress.

The public for the first time was finally aware of the neglect of military air power over the last decade. The public and political consciousness was aware of the scope and importance of civil air operations. When the military and civilian factors were coupled, it became possible to support the expansion of all facets of aviation. Although there was an interval before this effect became significant, the foundation for World War II air power had been laid, and the sacrifices had not been in vain.

THE MILITARY SITUATION

To appreciate how much the military programs had been degraded because of the Depression, it is necessary only to look at a few figures. Air Corps appropriations had been $38,892,968 for 1930–31 but only $25,673,236 for 1932–33. Sales of military planes and engines dropped from $17,167,794 in 1932 to $14,494,798 in

1933. The decrease in support for operations was about three times as severe as the reduction given procurement. Even at that, the number of planes procured amounted to only about half of what the previous programs had called for. The problems of recovering from the Depression were preeminent in public and political considerations, and the total number of people involved in aviation was insignificant in terms of total population and of economic impact. So it was natural that previous neglect had not attracted attention. The airmail incident, though short lived, received such wide publicity and aroused such intense emotional response that public concern for defense began to be felt.

As applied to all facets of military activity, the economic restraints of a depression economy were reinforced by a defensive attitude generally called "isolationism." This combination tended further to depress support in terms of appropriations and priorities. Such a defensive posture evolved into a defense strategy that colored all planning and tended to put aviation at the tail end of a tenuous line.

It may be difficult to appreciate the implications of such a point of view in the post–World War II era, where national interests span the oceans and where events in foreign countries assume equal news value with local items. George Washington's admonition to avoid foreign entanglements was taken seriously as a working doctrine in the 1930s. Defense implied that hostile action meant invasion, and this in turn meant an attack from the sea across the oceans. It also implied that strategic thinking was concerned primarily with *reaction* to a hostile move. This relieved planners of the necessity of contemplating offensive actions or excursions beyond our shores.

Part of the basis for this attitude was a long-lasting revulsion from the horrors of World War I. Part of it stemmed from the attitudes of large numbers of immigrants who had crossed the Atlantic precisely to escape the recurrent wars of Europe with their frightful tolls in human life and destruction. This was particularly strong in the Middle West, where enclaves of specific nationalities settled because they considered the United States a safe haven where they could live in peace. Part of it was a fringe effect from the distress of economic depression. Although we had defense responsibilities in Panama, Hawaii, and the Philippines, there was a generally held feeling that we had no colonial ambitions and these areas were not considered foreign possessions. We had foreign trade, but our preoccupation was with internal commerce. It was therefore hard to realize that our vital national interests could be seriously affected by foreign actions.

The sea was the path of attack, and the surface navy was the first line of defense. The Navy had the further responsibility of protecting the sea lanes to assure peaceful traffic. Traditionally, the Navy made a practice of "showing the flag" in foreign ports to impress others that the United States had the force to discourage seaborne adventures of hostile nature. In spite of the bombing exercises off the Virginia Capes in the early 1920s and the ambitions of the naval aviators, the naval doctrine gave precedence to surface elements and surface actions. This meant that carriers and airplanes tended to assume second priority until about 1927. After this, the carrier and its air complement became an ever-increasing element in Navy planning. The shipboard plane had early been recognized as an adjunct to the mission of the surface ship, but the striking power of the air element itself grew in importance.

There were similarities in the evolution of Army aviation. Coastal defense guns and forts were considered viable defense measures up to the early 1930s. Originally, the air arm had been part of the Signal Corps, and all planning related air action to the support of ground action. Command of the air was reluctantly acknowledged as necessary to prevent enemy air interference with friendly ground activity. The upstart aviators who espoused air action as effective in an independent role were suppressed or disciplined.

Although the Army Air Corps had been elevated by the Act of 1926 to the status of Air Corps with its own chief of corps, the general staff remained predominately ground-oriented in its thinking. This attitude persisted generally right up to the early days of World War II. It was even reported that, as late as 1940, President Roosevelt shared the Navy viewpoint that air action was inherently part of surface action. There were subtle but sound reasons for the Navy position. The naval forces were completely mobile themselves, and the point of contact with the enemy tended to be transient and remote. For protection and offensive action, it was natural to bring the air arm along and integrate it with the surface units. But in the long-range, ground-based air arm, it was illogical not to use the independent mobility of aircraft when coordinating it with a slow moving or stationary ground action.

A typical difficulty in penetrating the mass experience of World War II so that the prewar environment can be evaluated is the matter of public acceptance of the potential impact of air attack. With the bombing of Britain, Pearl Harbor, the Battle of Midway, and the air offensive against Germany and Japan, it seems perfectly clear that the potential for aerial attack should have been recognized. Saying that Pearl Harbor vindicated William Mitchell is not enough to clarify the situation.

THE VISIONARIES

General Mitchell is widely credited with being the hero and martyr of the struggle for recognition of the potential of air power. His campaign was noisy and flamboyant. Though his tactics were probably necessary, his claims and manner were definitely impolitic and tended to obscure the fundamental issue. A strong residual conflict colored military decisions and actions all through the period being considered.

Objectively, it must be recognized that the results of the bombing tests in 1921 were appreciated by many in a number of different quarters and that some segments of the Navy were not as backward in recognizing the significance as might be supposed. In the Army, there were many who continued the struggle and who were dedicated, forceful, and politically astute. In subsequent years, thanks to those Air Corps officers such as Benjamin D. Foulois, Henry H. Arnold, Frank M. Andrews, George Kenney, Hugh Knerr, James Doolittle, and others, the low-ranking Air Corps fared better than might have been expected. But funds and progress came hard. What appeared to be a question of doctrine was more probably a matter of money.

The 1922 *Aircraft Yearbook* of the Aeronautical Chamber of Commerce contains a summary of the 1921 bombing tests and the text of the report of the Aeronautical Committee of the Disarmament Conference. This should be required reading for anyone desiring to get the basic facts underlying the controversial issues.

It should be noted that the Navy cooperated in setting up the test and participated in the bombing. Some of the most cogent comments on the test came from Admiral William A. Moffett. The advent of airpower was recognized by the press, Congress, and the Navy, as well as by the Army and the Air Service. But there was *no agreement* that this implied the need for a separate Air Force or significant increase in the air arms. In fact, during subsequent years, overstatement of the issue implied the inclusion of Navy air and close-support Army air in any independent Air Force. This led to Army and Navy opposition. Congress immediately recognized that expenditures for battleships should be curtailed in favor of aircraft and air personnel, while the Navy saw that the need for many new large carriers was urgent. This translated into a congressional move to reduce funding right at the time the Navy needed more.

Some extracts from the account in the *Yearbook* are pertinent: "For the next three months intensive training was carried on by the naval and military aviators. There was keen rivalry and common interest. If there was any tinge of conflict, it was not among the airmen, but between the airmen of both services as a unit and the advocates of the capital ship as the 'backbone of the fleet.'" Among those on board the *Henderson* (the observer's ship) was Gen. Alford V. Williams, Army chief of ordnance. "A bomb was fired today," said he, "that will be heard around the world." Maj. Gen. Charles T. Menoher, who at that time was chief of the air service, said "A cold material fact has been demonstrated. The fact is that the battleship can be sunk by the aerial bomb." Admiral Moffett said "We must put planes on battleships and get aircraft carriers quickly. That is now the great need. We must now get them and quickly. We must put aviators on all our battleships to enable them to ward off air bombing attacks in the event of war, pending the time we get airplane carriers."

In view of the early recognition by the Navy of the potential of aviation, it is clear that the dissension that influenced the relations between Army and Navy and between airmen and surface forces was more than a ships versus air contention. Perhaps the underlying problem right up to World War II was the matter of distributing the military's limited funding. The aviators had attempted to show that ships were expensive and aircraft were cheap as justification for more generous support of aviation. Congress had picked up their argument as a possible means for cutting total funding by taking it out of support for the surface Navy. Within the Navy, there may have been serious differences of opinion as to carrier-based aircraft and individual shipborne aircraft. There would have been differences over the types of planes most suitable for different missions. But the possibility of being penalized financially for recognizing aviation undoubtedly obscured objective discussion.

THE ARMY AND THE NAVY

Between the Army and the Navy, there was the question of priority in the total national defense posture, with the Army being inferior. In contests with the Navy over "roles and missions," assignments, the Army General Staff, being predominately surface oriented, understood the surface Navy, and so the Air Corps suffered from being both Army and an adjunct to the surface forces. This became critical when the B-17 long-range bombers appeared. The Navy contended that aircraft of that range obviously had to work offshore in a defensive scenario and consequently were usurping an assigned Navy function. This was not semantic quibbling. It was a matter of control and direction of striking forces.

The low prestige of the air arms and their relatively small allocations of funding affected the industry by severely limiting both purchases of complete aircraft and support for research or development. In spite of past recommendations setting a minimum number of aircraft necessary for procurement, there was serious discussion at one time of limiting the Air Corps's annual procurement to 200 aircraft of one category only. Since the categories consisted of bombers, fighters, attack, and trainers or utility, this replacement once every four years would not have kept up with obsolescence and attrition. Fortunately, this concept was never put into practice, although the procurement rates did reach such low levels that the effect was almost the same.

One factor that alleviated the situation was the provision in section 10-(k) of the Army Five-Year Program of 1926 that read, in part: "The Secretary of War or the Secretary of the Navy may at his discretion purchase abroad or in the United States with or without competition, by contract, or otherwise, such designs, aircraft, aircraft parts, or aeronautical accessories of the best kind for the Army or the Navy."

Although competitive procedures were enforced during the whole period up to the war emergency, experimental and service test quantities of thirteen planes could be bought. This strategem was used judiciously to keep a trickle of development flowing. Obviously, funds had to be justified and appropriated even for these functions, but much of the competitive procedure could be avoided with a corresponding saving in time.

The industry, being on the verge of starvation and bankruptcy, was concerned that all its members fared equally. This attitude, combined with similar political considerations, tended to stress restrictive competitive laws, their interpretation, and regulations. It got particularly bad in 1935 and 1936 when, after the airmail operation, there was a concerted effort to correct past deficiencies. While not bad in the sense of insuring survival and providing the stimulus of competition, the restrictions and procedures limited the flexibility that was urgently needed to obtain the maximum rate of improvement in a nearly stagnant atmosphere. The same restrictions imposed severe penalties on the manufacturers who lacked the financial muscle to provide prototypes and to continue submitting bids many of which inevitably would be futile.

Within the military forces, the personnel strength was maintained at minimum levels. This was particularly hard on the junior air services. Since most of the force was, of necessity, assigned to the operating units, very few men were left for administrative, technical, and procurement functions. The number of senior officers who had grown up in aviation was even smaller, since they had to have entered the service prior to or very early in World War I. A large proportion of the senior ranks were held by officers who had transferred from other branches. Fortunately, they were usually gifted individuals who had overcome the natural difficulties of learning to fly under the tutelage of junior officers who were naturally skeptical of questionable benefits that resulted from accepting seniors without aviation experience.

The case of Wright Field illustrates how thin the staffing was. As the Materiel Division of the Air Corps, the field was responsible for engineering, laboratory operation, procurement, and the administration of the maintenance and supply depots. In the middle 1930s, ninety officers and about one thousand civilian personnel were on duty there. Included in these numbers were those involved in flight tests, experimental flight maintenance, operation of one of the major supply depots, and the operation of two flying fields. A project office, corresponding to a "class desk" in the Navy, acted as a coordinating point for engineering, procurement, and field operating problems. In this capacity, it was the key point for contact with manufacturers. A typical office for all bombers, for instance, consisted of one officer, one civilian engineer, and one stenographer.

The staffs in the headquarters in Washington were equally austere. Here, the responsibilities were much broader, covering personnel, funding, and the operation of the whole force. Added to these were the burdens of maintaining contact with Congress and handling the budget. The portion directly related to the materiel aspects was insignificant. Paradoxically, this apparent dearth of help was a distinct *advantage*. Lines of communication were short, so there was no chance to interrupt the relation between policy and action. Action, review, and approval were facilitated.

Short of formal competitions with all the specifications and prior notices, there were many contacts between contractors and the services that required consideration and action. A contractor could telephone or see the chief of Air Corps with a suggestion or request. The Air Corps chief could call the chief engineer or chief of 43 procurement at Wright Field with a policy directive or approval. Approval or change-order action could be initiated within a few hours. When necessary, two or three individuals could go to headquarters with all available information, sit in a conference with the chief or other high-policy-level officers, and return the same day both with a clear understanding of policy and with authority to proceed. The final documentation or contracts that resulted might fail to reveal the process by which agreement was reached; but the files were not cluttered, and subsequent review was unnecessary.

The relationships between industry and the services were equally direct. A project officer, even if only a lieutenant, could talk directly to the president of a company, and both had confidence that each could proceed on an agreed course. Maj. Oliver Echols, chief engineer at Wright Field, would frequently refer a president or chief engineer of a contracting firm to a project officer to handle the details of sometimes complex matters after having provided only informal guidance. While this expedited action, it made it difficult to retrace the course of a specific action or the factors involved.

OTHER FACTORS

One other aspect of aviation activity had a profound effect on progress and the posture of the United States at the beginning of World War II. This was the air-show, racing, and record-breaking activity. Both locally sponsored air shows and races and the famous National Air Races had attracted popular support and financed much development since the earliest days of flight. It is difficult to evaluate directly the technical or operational inputs, but innovative design involving all aspects of advanced performance found expression and spurred development in many fields. Planes like the Wedell-Williams, the Gee Bees, the Art Chester racers, and the Howard Hughes record-breaking cross-country plane now in the Smithsonian all were in the forefront of performance. The longer cross-country races stimulated development of more conventional commercial types like Benny Howard's DGAs and the Lockheeds, which were equally important in the whole picture.

The requirement for maximum performance was particularly a spur to engine development. "Souped up" racing engines always delivered more power than was indicated by the service ratings. This, plus the invaluable advances in fuel developments, served to raise the performance of each succeeding generation of service-type planes. The racing activity was a small but intense development and testing crucible.

There were other factors that had uncertain impacts on military aviation but were part of the overall atmosphere of the time. Of the many agencies established by the New Deal in 1933 to aid in recovery from the Depression, the Civilian Conservation Corps took in young men from cities where unemployment was high and formed them into camps doing conservation work in relatively remote areas. The camps were run by reserve officers brought in on active duty and supported by military bases. Officers from all branches of the military thus received training very similar to administrating military installations. The camp at Death Valley was composed of boys from Brooklyn who were awed by the spaces and the desert skies at night. March Field at Riverside, California, provided some air support and supply.

In 1933, President Roosevelt directed that 7.5 million dollars be diverted from Public Works Administration funds to the Navy for aircraft and accessories. It would probably be found that some of the other agencies, through financing assistance and other measures, contributed in various ways to the support of the aviation industry. It is doubtful if the total of these collateral inputs amounted to very much, but they must be considered because they were at least headed in a positive direction.

The engineering and procurement elements within both services were held in less esteem than the operational units; yet these technical elements were the ones working with an impoverished industry that struggled to provide increasingly effective and sophisticated weapons to meet the needs of the growing doctrine of air power being developed by military planners and flying units.

Air Power as a phrase was unfortunately interpreted in many places as synonomous with an independent *Air Force*. Actually, no working relationship or doctrine existed for the interaction of this hypothetical organization with surface forces. Even the doctrine for combined Army-Navy operation and control was indefinite right up through Pearl Harbor. Consequently, this controversial issue tended to assume undue importance and obscured the increasing capabilities of all air weapons, however they might be used.

The era between 1927 and 1940 represented a time when aviation was plagued by a multitude of outside influences, as well as the internal problems of the military. This served to draw the whole aviation community into a closer relationship. Certainly, there was little "fat" in any program, and the stress of poverty amplified the need to select only those programs that promised significant advance. The representatives of industries that supplied military equipment and their counterparts in the services worked as a team with the goal of getting the most performance for the nation with the minimum of wasted effort.

The internal conflicts in the services served, in some respects, to refine the final decisions and products. The final proof rested with the force actually created. To appreciate the character of the evolution that took place in the relatively short time of ten or twelve years, it is necessary to explore the process in some detail. It was not an easy time, but it was exciting and eventually satisfying for those involved.

III THE REQUIREMENTS OF WAR

When Karl von Clausewitz said about 150 years ago that war was just an extension of national policy and that the principles of warfare were simple but not easy, he expressed a basic truth that is as applicable to *air* warfare as to any other sort of combat.

Gustav Hamel and Charles C. Turner in a book published in 1914, and obviously written before World War I, said, "It is well to remember that the phrase 'command of the air' is meaningless until aeroplanes can account for each other in the air." Foreseeing the increasing technology and the problems of controlling ever more mobile combat elements, they also wrote, "Clearly the conquest of the air means the evolution of a type of soldier far more highly educated and finely organized than the world has yet seen." Perhaps *trained* would have been a better word than *educated*, but Hamel and Turner understood the essential differences between forthcoming air warfare and the typical surface warfare of the past. Obviously, from the earliest periods of aviation, the ocean of air was envisioned as a territory where mankind would exercise all his activities, including warfare, as rapidly as his technology would permit.

DOUHET'S THEORY

Giulio Douhet, in the 1920s, propounded his philosophy that the aerial bomber could wreak such havoc that a nation's "will to resist" could be broken. This concept, although controversial, was embraced by many, even though it implied a freedom of offensive action that might be unduly optimistic. It disregarded, to an extent, the intermittent nature of air attack and further implied an ability to maintain *pressure* that was unlikely to happen. It tended to discount the inevitable reactions and defensive moves of an enemy.

Douhet's doctrines did attract attention to the growing capabilities of military air. The possibility that such concepts might develop raised the question of defense against such attacks and the possibility of the "air war" developing. In under-developed situations against weak opposition, the premise seemed to be valid. Airmen striving always to improve their striking capability naturally tended to neglect the defensive role. A determined attack could always be pushed through, but the cost and the possibility of sustaining the effort over a period of time had to be considered. Against a determined enemy and in a fully developed situation, it would have probably been more realistic to consider *ability* to resist rather than *will* to resist.

While, to some, Douhet was a prophet who established the principle of air warfare that all others followed, a good case can be made that military airmen in all countries were reaching similar conclusions independently. Certainly, there were references to Douhet, and there were intellectual discussions of the morality of bombing civilian centers. However, there were many differences in the way air power developed in different countries. There were many common elements that in general coincided with the attack principles put forth by Douhet, but perhaps *coincidence* is the main theme.

The differences from country to country seem to have depended upon the age-old factors of goals of the leadership, geography, resources, technology, and attitudes of the controlling population. For instance, Hitler's aggressive goal to acquire control of adjacent territories meant occupation by ground troops, so it was natural that aerial targets would be in close support of the ground forces. Hence, the Stuka. Geography suggested that long-range air power was not needed. However, the independence of air action dictated a separate air force. England, recognizing the growing potential of air power, created a separate air force, but with a strong naval heritage it found some difficulty integrating the naval air elements with the surface navy. A recognition of vulnerability lent priority to defensive forces, hence Britain's outstanding fighter force. England, surrounded by water and with some need for longer range operations to implement strategic missions, developed larger bombers, but with a lower priority. The geography of Europe implied that mass bombing attacks could be accomplished by medium-sized bombers in large numbers, which was the German solution.

In the United States, the strongly held concept that air power was an adjunct of surface force kept alive a strong commitment to small- to medium-sized aircraft for reconnaissance and troop support. Perhaps, the existence of opposition to independent air attack caused a stronger reaction on the part of the air power supporters that resulted in stressing the larger long-range bombers. For a time, this attitude in the Air Corps resulted in a prohibition of bomb-carrying capability for fighters.

The principles expressed by Douhet acknowledged some need for defensive forces, but the assumed overwhelming power of what was later to be called "strategic air" tended to put all other types and all other missions in a lower priority category. An unrestrained interpretation of the Douhet thesis would have had profound effect on the requirements and support for other types. To some extent, this did occur, particularly with respect to fighters in this country.

Two aspects of the Douhet thesis deserve more attention, as they affected the thinking that led to detailed requirements for weapons and their installations. One was that a mass bombing attack could be pushed through in the face of *any* air opposition. Therefore, engaging other aircraft in the air was a waste of time and resources. This led to the concept that suitably armed bombers flown in mutually supporting formations could provide all the protection that was necessary or feasible. The earlier phrase "account for each other in the air" envisaged battles for control of the airspace, at least to the extent necessary to complete some particular mission. The test of battle did demonstrate that determined attacks could be driven through in spite of losses. But the battles did develop, and attrition on both sides determined the ability to mount recurring attacks and maintain the pressure necessary to gain a cumulative decisive effect.

The other proposition was that air attack with its own priority of surface targets was independent of the line of contact or the engagement of surface forces. Hence, it should be directed independently and coordinated only at a higher level equal to the top level of the surface forces. This led to a need for an independent Air Force.

Military aviation enthusiasts claimed that World War I aerial achievements proved that the air had truly become a battleground with all the implications applicable to any other scene of combat. But this was not generally accepted, and as a matter of national policy, air operations were considered a limited extension of age-old surface combat. The other side of the argument was that aerial action had not significantly   47 altered or affected any of the campaigns of World War I. So, incongruous as it seemed in the light of the increasing performance of military aircraft, the self-propelled free-flying airplane tended in much military thinking to be linked like a tethered balloon to ground strategy and tactics.

To the new breed of airman, World War I had simply hustled aviation through adolescence. Now that aviation was approaching maturity, the basic requirement was a completely new doctrine and inventory of equipment. But this disregarded the other side of Clausewitz's premise. If war was an extension of national policy, then preparedness in peacetime was also an extension of national policy. After a war, a nation generally reacts with economic readjustment and a surge in political and public interest in things economic and social, with military concerns placed at the bottom of its priority list. The postwar reaction of the 1920s was overtaken by the Depression; as a result, there was never any recovery from the original reaction until the eve of World War II.

AIRCRAFT BETWEEN THE WARS

It is noteworthy that all statements of the situation and, correspondingly, of requirements appear in almost identical terms during the period from 1922 to about 1938. Included in the reports of investigating boards and committees, as well as in statements by interested individuals, would be variations of "shortages of planes and personnel," "technical deficiencies," "insufficient combat-ready aircraft for defense," and "inadequate base for emergency expansion both industrial and military," plus similar recommendations for correction.

Warning signs were seriously neglected. Though some people were alarmed by these signals, their concerns were not translated into requirements for dealing with the growing potential of air power. The withdrawal of Italy from the League of Nations and its subsequent incursion into Ethiopia were only noted in passing. It seems incredible that in the early 1930s Italy was credited as being number one in air power and that this failed to excite political or public interest. Germany, taking advantage of the worldwide Depression, started rearming, and Hitler in his *Mein Kampf* expressed his aggressive intents. But even this led to more discussion than action.

War itself is, of course, a completely illogical process in which reason has given way to a blatant struggle for power, overweening greed, or sheer desperation. So it is difficult to apply logic and reason to the preparation for war no matter how peaceful or defensive a nation's policies may be. There is always a limit to the amount of reason and logic that a nation can present to restrain a hostile force. Consequently, some force "in being" has to be maintained to demonstrate determination and reinforce negotiations. But it becomes a matter of policy to determine the form or composition of this force and how much effort should be expended in its support. Generally, the Allied victors in World War I relegated these considerations to very low priority until Hitler started his moves.

So it was that, in the United States, military airpower coasted on a dwindling force flying obsolescent planes. Aside from the Jenny (JN-4) with its production of some 7,000 or 8,000 planes, the only other major WWI production had been the D.H.4, copied from the British but powered with the American Liberty engine. Incidentally, it seems strange that the D.H.4 and other aircraft of this size were considered bombers in view of the much larger European Handley-Page, Caproni, Gotha, and Sikorsky planes. A start had been made to copy at least the Handley-Page and Caproni for production in this country, but after the war ended, they never entered the inventory. The twin-engined Martin Bomber had been developed, and

48

four were left on order at war's end.

Lacking a firm requirement or doctrine befitting an American peacetime posture, some designs conforming to World War I tactical experience were initiated as follow-on versions of foreign combat planes. Notable was the Thomas Morse MB-3 that looked like a follow-on to the French SPAD but used a 300-h.p. Wright Hispano engine. This did enter the inventory. The LePère appeared, but its use was confined to experimental projects. The Vought VE-7 entered service as an advanced trainer, but because it was a fine airplane, it took over many utility missions and became the predecessor of many Navy types.

The de Havilland D.H.4, a British design built and flown by the Americans, was a dangerous airplane until it was redesigned to incorporate a relocated fuel tank, one-piece fuselage, and improved landing gear.

The Keystone B-5A was the last WWI-type bomber used by the Air Corps.

Though designated by the Army as a night bomber, the Martin (Curtiss) NBS-1 was the type used by Billy Mitchell to sink the ex-German battleship Ostfriesland, *thus demonstrating the feasibility of aerial bombing of naval targets.*

The twin–Liberty engined Martin Bomber appeared in production quantities in the early 1920s and was the first large American bomber. By 1929, it was superseded by the Curtiss B-2 and a series of Keystone bombers. These planes, together with Boeing and Curtiss fighters and Curtiss, Douglas, and Thomas Morse observation types, represented the postwar generation. Both the Navy and the Army Air Service had their own design and construction facilities, which developed a number of types of aircraft by translating current technology into what was considered new military requirements. The designs of Alfred V. Verville at McCook Field were particularly interesting in the high-speed category and perhaps suggested the evolution of future pursuit types. In general, however, the service activity provided a capability for experimental projects, though the inventory articles came from industry. Civilian and political pressure finally phased out the manufacturing capabilities of the services so that by about 1927, after the 1926 act took effect, various forms of competition and contract procurement provided physical articles to implement the changing requirements.

The war surplus types that had remained in service tended to obscure the requirement for newer forms, but they had largely disappeared by 1927. The JN-6H with the Hispano engine was still in use in the reserve units in 1929 but had ceased to influence the development of either doctrine or procurement. D.H.4s had been modified by Boeing and Atlantic (Fokker) with steel tube fuselages and forward gasoline tanks, but these had been relegated to intermediate training duties until 1932, when the last seven were assigned to the Twentieth Pursuit Group at Mather Field, California, where, after a short period as utility craft, they were used as ground-gunnery targets.

Looking at the types making up the entire Air Corps in the 1931 maneuvers, it is evident that the planes in service were still only modest improvements of the types used in World War I. The recognized need for complete and revolutionary replacement had been met only partially.

At this time, 1931, there was little concern over the lack of progress, because the planes were satisfactory individual articles and were improvements over their immediate predecessors. But specifications requirements showed only minor evolutionary changes in structure and performance. By comparison with foreign military types, they seemed to be competitive, but the new types were few in number. Until Germany started rearming, there was cause for impatience but not alarm. The disturbingly slow rate at which technological advance was being absorbed into American military aircraft became apparent only by comparing them with newer civilian transports and recent racing planes.

In addition to the models being procured for service use, there was a continuing flow of experimental prototypes. For any tactical type such as observation or attack planes, for instance, there were considerable time gaps between new models because funds were always limited, and the whole spectrum of functional types had to be protected. Few reached production status; in essence, they represented insurance against an unexpected need for expansion. Typical was the Boeing B-9, an all-metal cantilever monoplane that reflected Boeing's approach to the civilian transport market with the Monomail and the 247. When the P-26As went into production, two low-wing, all-metal, cantilever versions called XP-29s were built as experimental articles, but they were not procured in quantity. The XP-30, which was produced in limited quantity as the PB-2 by Consolidated, typified the low-wing, all-metal,

Designed by Alfred Verville late in World War I, the V.C.P.-1 offered a semi-monocoque fuselage and tapered wings. Despite its excellent performance, this plane was not produced.

The late 1930s saw the advent of a great variety of all-metal semi-monocoque aircraft, such as the Seversky SEV-3M-WW pictured here.

cantilever monoplane, which, with its retractable gear, was a modern type for its day. But this article represented a response to a questionable requirement for a two-man fighter. For some time, it had been thought that, if a rear-firing defensive gunner were included, a pursuit plane could give up some maneuvering capability and continue its attacks since its tail would be protected by the flexible rear gun and the plane would not have to manuever to avoid enemy attack from the rear.

Looking at the inventory of the Air Corps as it appeared in the 1934 airmail operation, it is evident that the replacement of the 1931 vintage aircraft was almost complete. However, the types just entering the service—P-26s, A-8s, A-12s, B-10s, 0-35s, and B-7s—indicated that progress was marginal, and many older-model planes were still in service. The overall requirement for their complete replacement by new types still remained.

The Navy's first big carriers, *Saratoga* and *Lexington*, had come into service late in 1927. They were 33,000-ton vessels but were allowed to exceed the 27,000-ton limitation of the Naval Limitation Treaty because of a special provision that had been included. According to the 1927 *Aircraft Year Book*, the Navy had, at the end of 1926, twelve battleships with one catapult each and ten scout cruisers with two catapults each. In addition to the float planes for the catapults of the conventional surface ships, the Navy needed complete complements of aircraft with wheel landing gears so they could be catapulted off the carriers' decks and could land into the ships' arresting gears.

With the advent of the new carriers, attack and defense missions began to assume increased priority. To satisfy its need for large bombs for attacking surface vessels, the Navy developed dive-bombing, with large single bombs carried on relatively small, single-engined planes. The torpedo, being a typical naval missile, was a natural candidate for adaptation to air delivery. Torpedo planes became a unique development in the Navy. Now that large numbers of planes could be carried, the defense of the carrier and accompanying ships could be provided by typical pursuit, or fighter, types. At first, these naval planes were very similar to corresponding Air Corps aircraft, though they were modified with equipment and structure to fit them for carriers. In some cases, the craft were substantively identical, for instance, the Boeing F-4B for the Navy and the P-12 for the Air Corps. Eventually, the Army and Navy fighter types diverged as the Air Corps adapted its planes to larger fields and improved runways, while the Navy concentrated on characteristics peculiarly suited

During the mid-1930s, the Consolidated P-30 (PB-2) was the only two-seat monoplane fighter to reach operational status with the Air Corps.

The Curtiss A-12 Shrike used several novel ideas in its construction, including smooth-skin, semi-monocoque construction and trailing edge flaps.

Boeing F4B-1 fighters stand ready for final assembly in Seattle, Washington, plant. In the background, Boeing Model 80s are being constructed.

to carrier-deck operation. But all military aircraft, whether for the Navy or the Air Corps, demonstrated a very restrained application of the state of the art.

As the civilian transports in the early 1930s absorbed the advancing technology, the military types suffered by comparison. Few military planes could match the performance of the newer, all-metal, unbraced monoplanes. When the Martin B-10 appeared in the inventory, none of the existing fighters could catch it or the transports. The utility of P-26A, a transition type, was severely compromised in an attempt to match the 200-mph speed that was demonstrated first in the civilian types and then in the new bomber.

OUTMODED CONCEPTS

Warfare from ancient times to early in this century was envisioned as a struggle for the occupation of geography by surface units; this concept had to be revised and changed before adequate air power could be constructed. The persistence of this old theory can be illustrated by an incident from World War I. On August 18, 1918, as the battle at Amiens began, airplanes in some numbers were used to fly over the battlefield area so that their noise could cover the noise of tanks advancing under reduced power.

This employment of airplanes to make noise was the approved solution to one of the problems at the Army Command and Staff School in the early 1920s. Even as late as 1930, there were aviators still smarting under this precept, which so sadly denigrated their faith in aviation and its potential.

Before the requirements for military equipment can be stated, it is desirable to establish missions and the performance necessary to accomplish them, since this is always guesswork. There is a natural tendency to stick to existing categories of aircraft and call for "just a little more performance." With technical products having long lead times, it is essential to have more specific projections relating to the time period in which they will be available. In the services and in industry, these projections were design studies based on extrapolations of the then existing technology. While these projections were useful for planning purposes, the implied requirements for future technical capability only intensified the evident shortcomings being considered at any time.

The normal practice after World War II was to state the threat of potentially hostile nations in terms of the performance and characteristics of weapons. This simple approach was not available prior to World War II; the determinations then had to be made for our weapons, because we had no identifiable enemies in the early 1930s and were concerned only with a defensive posture. Even if threats could have been presumed, there would have been serious shortcomings because the reactive approach almost always neglects consideration of the most efficient use of our own resources.

There were some procedures that established a sort of guidance. These included specifications pertaining to development articles and procurement competitions. Then there were the budget procedures, which indicated desired programs and received scrutiny at all levels up to the Congress, where fund approval amounted to endorsement. But the difference between what the aviators thought was a suitable program and what the senior military staffs and politicians considered appropriate was so great that forward planning had to be done within the services with little guidance and with little certainty of eventual adoption.

So it was that the service technical agencies, ably abetted by contractor's design studies, projected the state of the art into potential future operational capabilties. During the early 1930s, it was apparent that a complete revolution in design and constuction was taking place with very little being applied to military performance. Even in the mid 1930s, when the initial technical revolution had taken place, it was evident that at the rate of development then occurring, operational performance would be deficient by the early 1940s.

NEW AVIATION PROCUREMENT

Requirements for development and procurement developed in numerous and devious ways. By regulation, any statement of need from a using agency, if approved, became a directive for the development and procurement organizations. This was by no means automatic. Simple modifications of existing items offered no problems. But the more that basic doctrine was affected and that items became complex and expensive, the more difficult the approval process became. In practice, technical and procurement agencies extending the state of the art and improving existing articles frequently created de facto requirements.

The close relationship of contractors to the military services frequently led contractors to propose or build prototypes on speculation. The proposals tended to reinforce conclusions drawn from the continuing design studies made by the engineering staffs of the military services. These projections were part of the inputs that resulted in type specifications that were in turn part of the estimates of future requirements—for instance, in the case of fighters for the early and mid-1940s, it was estimated that single-engine types would need about 1,600 horsepower to be effective.

There were instances where the contractors researched tactical concepts and possibilities, coming up with proposals that had not yet been formulated as approved military requirements. This source was very real and valuable. For instance, Larry Bell scouted the Air Corps and proposed the multi-place fighter FM-1, while the Boeing B-17 and the Curtiss A-18 were outstanding examples of the complete proprietary prototype. In fact, it would be hard to find a single proprietary prototype that was not procured at least for experimental purposes. Many went on into limited or full-scale procurement through competitive procedures.

The inevitable pulling and hauling between operational desires and technical capabilities has always existed and always will. In a rough sort of way, the planners or operators stated the character and performance of the weapons that they believed were required of projected missions. The technical agencies indicated what could realistically be obtained. Since these positions almost never coincided, the reconciliation process kept a close, but not always cordial, relationship between the operators, the technical agencies, and the producing organizations.

The Air Corps Board, revitalized in the mid-1930s, represented the organizational approach to formulating or approving doctrine and technical specifications for procurement. This function became part of the formal orgnizational structure of the services and has persisted in varying forms. The board cooperated closely with the development and procurement agencies, and this cooperation was undoubtedly a significant factor in the major jump in performance and capability of the aircraft that appeared just before the war.

It would have been convenient if the abstract need, in terms of the types and numbers used by the investigative committees and boards, could have been related to approved doctrine, then translated into type specifications, and finally used as the basis for funded procurement in the approved competitive manner. But such an orderly process never occurred. Much of what became available for the war was the result of expediency and exception to the routine.

NEW DESIGNS

The projections of future possibilities by the services and industry spotlighted the increasing loss of ground due largely to the shortage of development funding over the extended period. It should be recognized that development is also a significant by-product of quantity procurement. Every article built reveals some feature that could be improved, and as these modifications are incorporated, there is steady progress without a need for specially oriented projects. From 1922 to 1939, there was very little quantity procurement of military types, so this input was limited. Consequently, a number of expedients were employed to keep development alive and to meet an implied requirement even when there was no formally approved requirement document.

There had always been the practice of changing models within a given type procurement. This included changes in engines and use of improved power models of the original engines. But some modifications were more extensive. A good example is the B-23. At the tail end of the B-18 production, by change order, a number of the last articles were to be redesigned to include more powerful engines and extensive configuration changes. This was done in the hope that the new model B-23 could be reordered over an extensive period without a break in production.

Then there were the classified, competitive projects for the big bombers that became the XB-15 and XB-19. These started as design studies at Wright Field during 1932 and 1933. Roscoe Wilson (Lt. Gen., USAF, Ret.), then a second lieutenant in charge of the design group, does not know where the original authorization started. There were a number of senior officers all thinking of air power and of independent air forces where long-range heavy bombers would be the key striking force. The original studies were referred to Washington for comment and then revised. They represented projections of the state of the art and particularly of the potential of power plants.

These projects were certainly not a response to any doctrine. Even in 1937 and 1938, the Army and the politicians did not concede a need for even the B-17, which was half the size of the B-15 and a quarter the size of the B-19. The Navy was strongly contesting the procurement of the B-17. It would probably be impossible to trace the inputs and persuasions that succeeded in getting approval and funding for such ambitious projects in 1934 and 1939.

Boeing, which had the B-15 project underway, built as a proprietary venture a four-engine bomber that was roughly a half-scale version of the B-15. It was entered in the Army competition for multi-engine bombers but lost after a crash prevented the completion of the required tests. After the accident destroyed the Boeing prototype entry, it was possible to negotiate immediately a service test contract so that the B-17 got a lower number than the B-18, which won the competition.

With fighters, the situation was much worse. Within the Air Corps itself, there was strong sentiment that fighters had very limited capability and that bombers would always have ascendancy in performance and would be capable of providing their own defense with independent action. At Wright Field in the design study groups and in the project office, there were convictions that high-performance small planes had as much relative potential as big bombers had, both for performance and for load carrying, if the power plants became available. However, the necessary power always seemed beyond the evolutionary expectancy. Based on projections and design studies, it was possible with the help of Gordon Saville, one of the two permanent members of the Air Corps Board, to get approval for the specifications for two advanced types. Secret competitions were held and resulted in the XP-38 and

the XP-39.

In addition to experimental competitions for the very advanced types, there were other steps taken to minimize the impact of limited development funding. The experimental programs went ahead based on the availability of high-powered engines, even though there appeared to be little possibility of their being available as soon as they were needed. For instance, the B-19 was laid out for the 2,000-h.p. Allison 3420, but the 1,700-h.p. Wright R-3350 had to be used to complete the airplane.

There had always been a requirement for transport aircraft, but the procurement of the C-47 was undoubtedly influenced by the desire to capitalize on civilian developments and to have military aircraft as good as the civilian types, even if they

As the basic transport of the Allies in World War II, the Douglas C-47, military version of the incomparable DC-3, provided yeoman service on every front.

Douglas B-18s were the standard medium bomber of the Air Corps in the late 1930s and did extensive service as coastal patrol aircraft during World War II. 57

were not specifically developed to projected military requirements. The B-18 series was a Douglas adaptation of the DC series and also capitalized on civilian development. The reverse process existed, too, of course. Military development, although limited in scope and application, bolstered development in industry regardless of direct application. Boeing transports and the later Douglas transports benefited for the big four-engine bomber programs.

For a long time, there was serious discussion whether bombers should be modified transports or transports should be modified bombers. Evidence of both trends existed and still does. In other combat types, there were no civilian counterparts, and the final solutions had to be service-supported. However, aerodynamic, structural, and propulsion components were common, so some cross-fertilization applied even here. But the increasing size and power of the radial air-cooled engines, while acceptable in larger planes, became disadvantageous in fighters, restricting both vision and performance. So the development of the liquid-cooled engines continued with projected powers in the 1,000-h.p. range.

In the mid-1930s, the estimated growth rate of the air-cooled engines had to be based on the funding rate, which could not be expected to change. Most, if not all, of the foreign high-performance planes used liquid-cooled engines, and the development of liquid-cooled configurations enabled the United States to make use of the more highly developed Rolls-Royce engines after the war began.

AN AWAKENING

The projected requirements and the sluggish growth ceased to be an academic concern as Germany rearmed and the Messerschmitts set speed records. The British development of the Spitfire added fuel to the catch-up drive, and by 1939, as the war clouds gathered and reports such as Lindbergh's on the German Air Force filtered into U.S. political consciousness, the pressure to overcome the past became intense.

The tactical schools and senior air officers' individual statements before the investigative committees formed a sort of broad guide. When the phrase "10,000 pounds, 10,000 miles" was used in the mid-1930s to describe the desired capabilities of future bombers, it was a long way from being a specification. However, even the early B-17s ran into opposition, partly from the residual abhorrence of military forces, partly from concerns with other social and political matters, and partly from the problems associated with reconciling priorities within the military.

A similar cliché related to fighters, "400 mph, 4,000 pounds, 400-h.p.," was equally imprecise. It did indicate a performance level that appeared to be necessary, but the weight and power were variables that could not be fixed by semantics. The XP-38, appearing in early 1939, demonstrated that somehow a capability had been developed to create the competitive performance. Its 400 + -mph speed at 20,000 feet was outstanding and reassuring. But its weight was over three times that of the semantic dream, and its power was five times greater.

The XB-15, which came out sooner, attracted more attention than the XB-19, which was probably more significant in the total picture of air power. But the B-17, a derivative of the XB-15, had the most immediate and significant impact on the ensuing war.

DEVELOPMENT OF WEAPON SYSTEMS

It is normal in summarizing the development of weapon systems to use their overall performance to describe the process. But it is wrong to assume that these data automatically include the development of the components that make the whole.

Consider the "type specification," which is the basis for the "detail design specification." The type specification includes: bombs, guns, instruments, wheels, brakes, oxygen systems, crew locations and accommodations, servicing requirements, materials, processes, finishes, standard radiators, fittings, nuts and bolts.

Then there were fuels and lubricants; propellers, radios, and electrical systems; and standards for strength and for operational conditions such as winter and desert exposures. The same shortages that precluded getting complete operational articles handicapped component development as well. The steady evolution of the components is apt to be taken for granted, but in general it was as difficult to achieve as was the development of fighting articles. Some of it was combined with the procurement of experimental flight articles, and some was a by-product of civilian development. But part of it was just a case of interested and dedicated individuals both in the service and in industry recognizing a need and going ahead with or

A modified P-36A, the Curtiss XP-42 was equipped to test several engine cowlings.

without specific authorization and within the limitations of austere budgets.

Guns and turrets illustrate some of the points. The .30- and .50-caliber Browning machine guns had been standard in the United States as ground guns and available as air guns since the middle 1920s. There was steady development to improve their functioning and increase their rate of fire. However, the Air Corps standard was two .30-caliber machine guns, later modified to two .50-calibers. It remained for the British use of eight guns early in the war to stimulate the need for more firepower.

Early combat experience indicated the need for increased firepower, for self-sealing fuel tank protection, and for armor-plate protection for crews. This requirement was formalized by Gen. "Hap" Arnold at the same meeting in headquarters at which he raised the spares question. After a briefing on the situation, Arnold stated unequivocally that we would include these features immediately. So much for formal requirement statements and documents.

In the spring of 1940, I accompanied Col. Carl Spaatz to England. We were assigned as observers to the American Embassy in London, where we met with Group Captain Sorely to discuss armaments. Sorely appears to have been the proponent of the multi-gun configuration for fighters. In response to a query from Spaatz about the relative suitabilities of the .50-caliber and .30-caliber guns, Sorely stated that the United States was fortunate in having the option of choosing one or the other. The British had *no* capability of getting .50-caliber weapons into produc-

Propelled by a massive 2,000-h.p. Pratt & Whitney R-2800 engine and armed with eight .50-caliber machine guns, the Alexander Kartveli–designed Republic P-47 Thunderbolt was one of the most powerful fighters of the Second World War.

tion, and since they had to make do with .30-caliber guns, they decided on the eight-gun minimum. He further described in great detail the difficulties of introducing a new caliber into a combat situation. The .50-caliber alternative was being skipped in favor of a 20-mm. cannon sometime in the future. (The British equivalent of our .30-caliber was called Browning .303.)

The small pursuit airplanes originally designed for two fuselage-mounted guns had difficulty absorbing multiple guns in the wings because of structural and space problems. As might be expected, there were some variants. One solution in the P-40s was to use two fuselage guns and four wing guns; placing six .50-caliber guns in the wings was considered acceptable and equivalent to eight smaller guns. The P-47 could accommodate eight .50-caliber guns in its wings, while the P-38 started out with four .50-caliber guns and the 37-mm cannon giving it built-in carrying capacity.

With both the P-38 and the P-39, which had a cannon and two .50-caliber guns, the probable inadequacy of the two-machine-guns "standard" requirement had been anticipated. The proposed type specifications for the two-engine and single-engine interceptors called for the increased armament. The Air Corps Board concurred with the increase, thus effectively requiring it for the experimental types. This increased armament provision was initiated about four years before the World War II battle experience dictated the necessity for all fighter types.

The cannon called for in the FM-1, the P-38, and the P-39 was originally the Colt-manufactured standard Ordnance Dept. 37 mm. This was a ground gun, loaded by hand with five round clips. The FM-1 required a gunner in each of the nose nacelles to load the guns. With the fighters, it was necessary to develop a magazine and an automatic feed. Colt failed initially in this effort, so it was made part of the experimental airplane contract for the aircraft manufacturer to devise such a feed. Subsequently, separable links were devised to form disintegrating belts. Drums and magazines were developed, plus a continuous belt in a horseshoe-shaped track. But these were later and the 37 mm, while used in the P-39, was dropped in favor of the standardized 20 mm. in the P-38 and other fighter installations.

Flexible guns for defense seem to have evolved more by stages than by specific direction. As long as open cockpits existed, .30-caliber hand-held guns were operated by the gunner from a flexible mount not very different from World War I mounts and were aimed by "iron sights" with a forward vane to provide some crosswind compensation. The forward gun in the Martin B-10 was mounted in a rotatable shield that suggested the form, at least, of future turrets.

The Martin B-10 was the first U.S. bomber to mount a fully enclosed gun turret.

Of more than 9,500 P-39s built by Bell in Buffalo, approximately 4,000 were supplied to the Soviet Union by Lend-Lease.

Somewhere along the way, as the all-metal structures came into use, it became apparent that the .30-caliber bullet, at least from one or two guns, was inadequately destructive. The high-impact loads on the mounting structure for machine guns must be appreciated to realize that going to .50 calibers in a flexible mount was difficult. The Bell Aircraft Company developed a small shock-absorbing adapter to go between the gun and the structural mount, which greatly reduced the structural loads for fixed or flexible guns. The .50-caliber gradually became the standard gun for fixed and flexible mounts.

But where the fixed guns could use detached magazines holding a large number of rounds with short connecting chutes, the flexible guns required different solutions. Magazines attached to guns were heavy and not only restricted the number of rounds that could be fired without reloading but also made swinging and aiming difficult. Flexible chutes and remote magazines had to be developed. Even after electric and hydraulic turrets were available, there were many installations, such as the waist gun positions in the bombers, that were hand held and aimed.

Although some flexible gun enclosures were called turrets, the first powered turrets were specified for the XB-19. Two turrets accommodated a 37-mm. cannon and a .30-caliber gun. Another turret mounted a .50-caliber gun. This was an early start on the development of the powered turret, which was so valuable in a variety of planes in World War II.

The interest in cannon with explosive projectiles had arisen early. There are many examples of experimental installations of numerous different types and calibers. Hispano Suiza had built a cannon engine by the end of World War I. In this arrangement, a cannon was mounted in the vee of the engine, with the barrel projecting through the propeller shaft and the gearbox. By the early 1930s, interest in "shell guns" was fairly intense in Europe, and though it was less so here, the guns were still not neglected or overlooked.

As noted before, the 37-mm. Browning by Colt was available and modified for aircraft use. There was some development on guns of .9-inch bore here, but they never reached production status. Overseas, there were several types in a variety of bores. The 20-mm. was considered the smallest capable of using a fused projectile, while the 37-mm. was considered the largest adapatable to completely automatic fire. To name a few of the European cannon that merited attention, there was the Bofors 20-mm in Sweden, which became available in 1938; the Madsen 23-mm. from Denmark, of which four were acquired for testing in the United States; the Oerliken 20-mm. in Switzerland, although the company had close connections to the Germans; the Rheinmetall in Germany; and the Hispano Suiza in France. There were others, of course, but the Madsen, the Oerliken, and later the Hispano Suiza were probably the only ones seriously considered.

Hispano Suiza had picked up the Oerliken but soon developed its own 20-mm. In 1937, the British obtained rights to reproduce it, although more than two years passed before manufacturing capacity was created and the bugs were worked out. The United States arranged a contract to reproduce this gun late in 1939, and deliveries started late in 1941. Although both the British and American guns had a common origin, there were differences arising from manufacturing techniques and from different ideas of correcting difficulties. By 1943, the two versions were brought close enough to be considered standardized.

The armament configurations of all aircraft in all services seems to have followed a number of extraneous factors rather than a formally determined policy or doctrine. Of course, the variables influencing selection of weapons are numerous. There is basically the weight of projectiles that can be delivered in a very short time at a fleeting target. The susceptibility of the target to damage from different weights and types of projectiles may determine in certain missions or theaters the type of weapons used and certainly the type of ammunition employed. Each aircraft has its own structural and carrying capability problems. Considering that a .30-caliber gun weighs about 30 pounds, a .50-caliber one weighs about 60 pounds, a 20-mm one weighs about or just over 100 pounds, and a 37-mm gun weighs a little over 200 pounds, the effect of choosing different guns cannot be taken lightly.

But guns and bombs have to be aimed. For years with the open cockpit fighters, the "iron sights" were a bead and ring mounted on top of the cowling on a tube resembling a shotgun barrel. With higher speeds and closed cockpits, optical sights were developed to project a lighted ring and a bead on a "see-through" reflector. The image projected through a collimating lens eliminated parallax so that the dot of the bead appeared to stay on the target out in space in spite of some movement of the gunners sighting eyes. The next step was to include compensation for relative movement between the firing platform and the moving target.

For flexible guns, some sort of fire-control system was needed. In brief, this combined the functions of the optical sight with computed compensation and eventually provided remote or servo traversing of the guns. Incidentally, the XFM-1 included an embryonic fire-control system to sight and control the forward-firing 37-mm. cannon. This advanced component was included in this 1937 project.

In the mid-1930s, the Norden bombsight was developed; this device gave superior performance and permitted the development of the precision bombing technqiues that became so significant. It will be seen that these ancillary programs together with many others existed long before the emergency. While reference to specific demands for these technical requirements may never be found, it is clear that without their continuing development the complete weapon systems would not have achieved their full military capability.

Bombs also have development problems. There are many different sizes for different purposes. Aerodynamically, some bombs that are stable at one speed of release may be unstable at another, even going so far as to fly back up at the airplane. Fins and shape require research. Then, there are fuses in a wide variety. Although the requirements for guns and bombs seem reasonably apparent, there are similar

First flown in September, 1937, the Bell XFM was intended as a bomber interceptor, though it did not reach production.

ones for radios, cameras, oxygen systems, instruments and automatic pilots, parachutes and personal crew equipment (electrically heated suits, for instance), bullet-proof glass, and armor plate. The more complex the military airplane and the higher the performance, the more numerous the components and the more demanding the technical sophistication of these elements, which in fact determine the machine's capabilities perhaps even more than the configuration and power of the vehicle do. These self-evident truths become ever more significant with time and apply to the future more definitely than to the 1930s and World War II.

The only unique aspect of guns and armaments in aircraft is their adaptation to the aerial vehicle. The history of a particular gun or armament development is frequently independent of any use in aircraft, since the possible uses of arms are limitless. A torpedo is used in submarines, fired from surface vessels, and dropped from aircraft. The same rapid-firing gun used for anti-aircraft may be installed and fired from planes. So in considering the period just before World War II, any interest in the specifics or details of aircraft armament has to be pursued in the armament field. Nevertheless, it must be recognized that the airplane as a vehicle is simply a means of bringing to bear the potency of arms. Vehicle performance and armament performance need to be combined to ascertain a weapon's potential impact.

AIRCRAFT RANGE

The effective range of a weapon is one of its important performance characteristics. In the case of the military airplane, this becomes the range, or better the combat radius, of the airplane itself. In the United States, the possible size of the radius of action seemed to be unique. Without question, geography had a real influence. At one time, the justification for our emerging heavy bomber capability was that these aircraft could be used to reinforce or support the Panama Canal, Hawaii, Alaska, and the Philippines. With the number of long-range bombers available prior to the war, this was not very meaningful, but the argument revealed that the United States thinking automatically included ideas of long-reach aircraft influence. The very size of the nation on this continent required provision for extended ferrying range, if not for actual combat. No other nation except Russia had the same problems. Even Russia was mostly concerned with the European heartland, being separated from its eastern frontiers by Siberia. Peacetime manuevers for the United States involved deployment from Michigan to Florida, from one coast to the other, from arctic climate to deserts, and from sea level to the high plains and mountain areas. Automatically, these factors were ground into the concepts that came out as requirements or as type specifications. Beyond the formalized statements, designers, manufacturers, procurement agencies, and operators evaluated the suitability of aircraft and their components in these terms. Even the civilian airline developments involved coast-to-coast capability with fairly long intermediate hops.

All that is necessary to appreciate the impact of these distances is to compare some of our distance within the geography of Europe. New York to Los Angeles, if measured off from London or Berlin, would include all of Europe including Russia to the Urals, and the northern half of Africa including the Suez and about half of the Red Sea. This is not to say that other designers in other countries did not appreciate the range potential of aircraft or that other countries were not making long-range flights. English flights to South Africa and Australia were certainly long enough, and there were any number of foreign transoceanic flights. But in terms of national defense and support of ground combat, the distances involved were about what would have been considered the local flying area for military flying personnel in the United States.

Not only was ferrying range an inherent part of all concepts of our employment of aircraft, but also the wide variation in the environment in which they were operated fundamentally influenced the standards by which they were created. Sequential planes coming from a factory might be assigned to Alaska or Panama, Florida or Arizona. When gathered for maneuvers, they might mass in Louisiana or New England in the winter. Cold weather testing was done on new articles in Fairbanks, but gunnery contests might be held on Muroc Dry Lake or Honey Lake north of Reno. The planes automatically included provisions for operating in any or all of these surroundings. That versatility was unique in this country.

This inherent characteristic was brought home clearly when I had occasion to take a Spitfire Mark V from Wright Field in Ohio to Los Angeles and back. Because of its limited range, it was necessary to land at a number of little-used intermediate fields. The cooling on the ground at some fields was inadquate to permit taxiing from landing to the servicing area or from the hangars to the takeoff end of the field. Long runways on high altitude desert fields involved crosswind taxiing where the brakes faded away and required readjusting. The marginal stability that added so much to the superb maneuvering of the plane for combat and short flights became tiring and uncomfortable on long flights in rough air. The plane that was superior in all respects in its own country would not have met our standards or been accepted, unless modified, when evaluated by our acceptance and evaluating boards. The Spitfires going to Africa had an additional radiator. The other side of the picture has to be revealed too. Our planes were not considered desirable when evaluated abroad, where the adaptability bred into them had no real significance.

But, of all the characteristics, range was the most apparent factor. With bombers, there had always been a recognition of the trade-off of bomb load and fuel. Early in the war, there were incidents where the trade-offs were not clearly appreciated. It was possible to schedule missions that called for both maximum range and full bomb load simultaneously. If the bombs were carried, the planes could not return to base. If the full range was achieved, no bombs could be carried. While these extreme situations soon disappeared, there were still situations when some craft failed to reach home and when some missions involved alternate refueling stops on return.

RANGE FOR FIGHTERS

But it was not the long-range capabilities of the big bombers that was surprising. Within seven months after Pearl Harbor, P-38s were flying across the Atlantic to England. Soon, fighters were accompanying bombers on deep penetrations into Germany, and their appearance over Berlin added an element of consternation to the Luftwaffe's defense problems. Fighters flew the length of the Aleutians, operated over long ocean spans in the Southwest Pacific, and eventually appeared over the Japanese homeland. This potential or latent capability had been largely overlooked.

There were probably three reasons for obscuring the possibilities. One was partly the Douhet thesis that assumed that the pursuit function was insignificant; this was intensified in the United States by the efforts to create the bombing force against strong opposition and at the expense of the pursuit. Another was the Army position that air power was unimportant beyond about 200 miles from the front lines, and any pursuit would either provide ground support or keep enemy air from interfering with ground action. Further, it was felt that heavily armed bombers could provide "mutual support," which would make fighters unnecessary. There was no real doctrine existing that pertained to the small, maneuverable offensive plane, and certainly during the evolution of the later configurations of these types, there was no scenario envisioning the role they were to play in history.

By the end of the 1920s, carrying external belly tanks with auxiliary fuel was accepted practice. The Curtiss biplane Hawks, the Boeing P-12s and F4Bs, and observation types such as the Curtiss Falcons were all equipped with attachments that alternatively accommodated racks for light bombs that weighed twenty to fifty pounds or the belly drop tanks. It became standard to consider that in addition to the normal fuel load, whether specified as endurance or range, about half of this amount could be carried as overload or auxiliary fuel. With the P-26A, the struggle for higher speed and performance dictated that this extra fuel above the load for the "design point" would be carried in internal tanks. Actually, it was common to service these auxiliary tanks routinely as though they were for normal fuel. The internal auxiliary fuel tankage continued up through the first generation of planes used in the war, P-40s to P-51s.

At the same time that auxiliary tankage became internal, there was a prohibition against external bomb racks. Part of this was to reduce drag and weight, and part was to avoid the possibility of Army ground commanders considering the fighters for close support missions. The Navy did not follow this course and even had a category, scout-bomber, that alternatively could use extra fuel for longer range on scouting missions or carry a bomb for attack missions.

Curtiss built Navy SBs at the same time that it was building P-36s. Burdette Wright, who at the time was president of the Airplane Division of Curtiss-Wright, had been an Air Corps officer and had a good understanding of Air Corps operations. Wright offered to install an external tank, probably one of the SB tanks, on a P-36 for test and evaluation. This proposal was accepted immediately by Wright Field, and the airplane so equipped was sent to the GHQ Air Force at Langley Field for consideration. The proposal to so equip P-36s was rejected unequivocally. Part of the reason was that external tankage on retractable landing gear planes increased the fire hazard, and part was a reaffirmation of the prejudice against external loads. So up to our entering into hostilities, the formal record, if any really existed, followed the concepts established with the P-26 in 1933 and 1934.

Initially the loser to the P-35, the Curtiss P-36 had a superior design and quickly supplanted its competitor as the primary pursuit plane of the Air Corps in the late 1930s. It was the immediate forerunner of the Curtiss P-40.

The Curtiss A-3 Falcon was similar to the 0-1B except for its bomb racks and additional machine guns in the lower wings for ground-attack purposes.

When I returned from England in July 1940 after a tour as "observer" and again assumed my role as pursuit project officer, it seemed to me that there was a distinct possibility that we might have to fly *all* our combat planes to active theaters since surface transportation by sea was becoming so uncertain and the distances in Europe were getting longer due to the loss of France and its airports. Approaching the pursuit contractors, I suggested that we were going to need a 2,000-mile ferrying range, but in view of the prohibition in external tankage, there could be no contractual coverage. This meant that the capability had to be investigated and design accomplished without compensation. Lockheed accepted the challenge immediately, but Republic balked.

There may be no documentation covering the next step. As this is being written in 1980, none of the remaining participants seems to have a clear recollection. The P-40Cs delivered in the early spring of 1941 had provision for 52-gallon belly tanks. Whether this stemmed from Curtiss arrangements with the English to make P-40s for the Royal Air Force, from Burdette Wright's continued interest in the belly tank project, from support from some of the active pursuit commanders such as William E. ("Bill") Kepner (later commanding general of the Eighth Fighter Command), or from informal requests to provide provisions for extended range is uncertain. With the loss of internal fuel capacity due to self-sealing tanks, the use of external tankage may have just sneaked back without being noticed.

What is definite is that the day after Pearl Harbor a radio communication from the Philippines requested information on the bomb rack installation of the P-40s stationed there. It noted that the bomb shackles could, of course, accommodate bombs, but there were no provisions for arming the bombs when they were dropped. Arming would have been accomplished by a cockpit control of a latch on the bomb shackle that engaged the arming wire—the wire was pulled out of the fuse to make the bomb live. I remember the reply vividly. The bomb shackle was incidental to the tank installation but arming provisions were part of a bomb carrying capability that was not approved.

There had been questions raised about the use of the bomb shackles to carry tanks. This was answered by the project officer, who stated that the standard bomb shackles were the only available mechanism developed and tested that provided standard attachment and reliable carrying and release. Another sidelight arose in 67 connection with the installation on the P-39. Although the tanks could be carried, there was inadequate clearance between the low fuselage and the ground for bomb fins. A change proposal from Bell for modification amounted to about $1,300 per plane and was disapproved because it was a bomb-carrying provision.

At a meeting with Generals Arnold, Spaatz, and Echols in January of 1942, I was asked what could be done to ferry fighters to England. It just happened that the drop tank installations on the P-38 had been flown 2,200 miles by Milo Burcham in their last test. This was the result of Clarence L. ("Kelly") Johnson's energetic pursuit of the "informal" suggestion. General Arnold wanted to know who authorized this program. I had to reply that it had not been authorized and that it still was not permitted. When he wanted to know how long it would take to install tanks, I estimated that it would take 90 days to start modifying aircraft that had already been delivered. When he asked what was going to take so long and finally said "get going," a new requirement existed. Sample Lockheed pylons and tanks were made available to others and from then on there were a number of solutions, which varied with individual plane types.

The use of standard bomb shackles meant that different sizes of tanks were interchangeably usable. There were 52-gallon, 108-gallon, 150-gallon, 300-gallon, and probably other sizes as well. The smaller tanks did not provide very low ferry range, but they all extended combat utility to some degree. Maximum ferry range was attained at a maximum cruise power that gave relatively slow airspeed. Since active operations usually involved higher speeds, and since the attainable range decreased markedly with speed, there was no specific figure for the radius of action in a combat situation. Further, if enemy engagement took place, the tanks were jettisoned even though the fuel had not been completely used. But the use of the unprotected external fuel for any portion of a particular mission added proportionately to range.

The potency of this alternative load can be appreciated by realizing that a 150-gallon tank was roughly the equivalent of a 1,000-pound bomb and that a 300-gallon tank equaled a 2,000-pound bomb. At the same time that the 150-gallon tank was developed for the P-38, and that two were used for the 2,000-mile range, a 300-gallon tank was developed. Two of these gave a ferry range of over 3,000 miles. A single 300-gallon tank reportedly was carried on one side and a bomb on the other in some Southwest Pacific missions. In Europe, a few missions were flown with two 2,000-pound bombs on P-38s. While heavy bombing was not the primary mission of the fighters, the provision for this utility involved very little penalty in weight or complexity and substantially none in performance.

Although occurring later in 1943, one step remained to complete the picture of range extension. General Kepner reports that, when he was ordered to England, General Arnold called him in and gave him the following instructions: Arnold wanted the fighters to be able to reach Posen in Poland from England. He wanted the fuel in internal tankage so that the planes could fight and get back after dropping their external fuel tanks. Adding more external fuel to what was now being carried was not satisfactory. Kepner was to go to the factories and see what could be done. At North American, a study indicated that a rear fuselage tank could be installed with some rearrangement. At Lockheed, it was determined that the leading edges of the wings could be made into fuel tanks if a core-type intercooler was put in the nacelles. The fuselage tank in the P-51, being aft, adversely affected the center of gravity and stability, leading to some unpleasant handling characteristics when the tank was full, but the forward-leading edge tanks of the P-38 made little difference. This was almost the end of the evolution. It still remained for the P-47N to be built as

a long-range fighter.

It will be seen that what had always been a technical possiblity became a reasonable alternative as the fighter got heavier and the power became available. Range depends upon efficiency (the ratio of lift to drag) and the percentage of the gross weight devoted to fuel. Consequently, the effort to reduce drag to attain high speed also improved basic efficiency. By overloading the maneuverable fighter, the heavier structure and power for maneuvering in combat became a smaller portion of the total weight, and the increased fuel raised the percentage of the total new weight to approximate that of bombers. As fighters used the overload fuel, the only penalty remaining was the tank-carrying mechanisms and the piping.

THE POTENTIAL AND THE NEED

The potential had been there all along, but there had been no obvious reason to develop it. General Arnold's desire to have fighters engage the enemy at a distance equivalent to that from Washington, D.C., to St. Louis bore little relation to the prewar concept that these planes should not get farther than 200 miles from the Army ground troops. The desire to get more than 2,000 miles of ferry range would have had no meaning in the 1930s, when defense strategy assigned the Navy all offshore responsibility. A specific requirement expresses only one illustrative example of a many-faceted capability. The total technical capability had to be considered, even though there was no specific need for its use.

If a requirement is considered to be a recognized need, the key word is *recognized*. It makes little difference where or by whom. Certainly before World War II, need existed in many areas and was stated in many places and in many ways. But the formal recognition at many times seemed to deny the need. However, even positions that seemed to oppose progress had the effect of requiring reexamination of proposals and rejustification of their validity. Coincidence of results suggested parallel but independent efforts that were possibly more influential than an orderly administrative process, which was frequently lacking, would have been.

During the preparation of this material, discussions with Donovan Berlin on the origins of the XP-40 illustrated this coincidence. He was chief engineer at Curtiss and was responsible for the P-36 and P-40. The P-40 in its thousands had a significant impact on the war, even though it was both praised and maligned.

Numerically the most important American fighter of the early war years, the Curtiss P-40 fought successfully in every major theater despite its obsolescence.   69

Having been the pursuit project officer at the time, I was certain that the Air Corps had requested Curtiss to modify a P-36 by installing an Allison engine to provide full-scale evidence of the benefits or disadvantages of liquid versus air cooling. Berlin, on the other hand, was convinced that Curtiss had initiated the program to get Allison to increase the altitude performance of its engine and thus to provide a plane that would win the next procurement competition. These apparently conflicting positions were reconciled easily when Berlin said, "I've always wondered why our proposal was approved so quickly." Probably, Allison was also prepared to pursue any modification that promised the possibility of quantity procurement to offset its large development investment.

Regardless of how the results were achieved, the quality of the aviation products that were developed represented competititve performance plus adaptability, versatility, and utility that were unique for the time.

Among the many records held by the author was a speed mark of 353 mph, set on October 26, 1938, flying a Curtiss P-36A between Wright Field, Ohio, and the Curtiss factory in Buffalo, New York.

70

IV THE BEGINNINGS
OF
MILITARY AIRCRAFT

The stone streets of Pompeii are rutted from the rims of chariot wheels. The spacing of the ruts is the same as our standard rail gauge, until recently our standard automobile tread, and the tread of ox- and horse-drawn wagons. Perhaps, wagons were put on rails, and autos first ran on rails, and trains when new had to use already established roadbeds. But automobiles ran on flat, smooth roads for years before the "wide tread" was introduced to improve ride and handling.

When a modern diesel locomotive followed by a 100-car train goes by, it is intriguing to reflect that its width is based on the beam width of the after end of a horse, which was an established standard going back 2,000 years.

In aircraft, going back a few years takes one into the realm of dreams instead of reality. Nevertheless, there are traces of concepts originating in the earliest days of flight that have significance right up to the age of space exploration. Many basic considerations became traditional and are applied to all aircraft. Some had profound effects on the characteristics of World War II aircraft.

Philosophical speculation offers the interesting hypothesis that manned military aircraft employed like cavalry in large masses as mobile force may have peaked in the World War II era and will be reinforced if not supplanted by different and more powerful weapons operated above the earth's surface. The aircraft may have an extended age of usefulness. But with the possibility that an historical peak may have already passed, it is worthwhile to consider the aircraft of World War II not only as individual examples of transient technology but also as part of a continuing history, starting with man's first flight and embodying basic concepts and precepts that extend beyond any single date in history

POST WORLD WAR I

By 1919, aviation development as illustrated by the types of aircraft in existence, which were developed in the last stages of hostilities or were coasting on the momentum of the war effort, indicated a strong promise for the immediate future. Large aircraft such as the 30,000-pound Handley-Page four-engine bomber suggested that the next generation would be impressive. But it was about fifteen years before this capability again appeared in military inventories.

By 1919, bombers, about half the size of the giants, were in existence in large numbers and varied types. In the United States, the Martin twin–Liberty engined bomber was a good example; aircraft of this type became the primary U.S. bombers for at least ten years.

High speeds for the fighters were crowding 200 mph, but here again it was about fifteen years before this high performance was available in service.

In the early 1920s, development turned to racers and progressed rapidly. Large-size development was applied to civil transport types. The economics of racing and

The American bomber program began with World War I types such as the Handley-Page 0/400. This example was built by the Standard Aircraft Company of Plainfield, New Jersey.

the early phases of civilian transport limited the amount of effort that could be applied.

Engine development had proceeded from about 80-h.p. rotary engines at the beginning of the war to around 200-h.p. liquid-cooled in-line engines for small planes and similar 400-h.p. engines for larger ones. There was a scattering of experimental engines coming into existence in the 500- to 600-h.p. class and some indication of experimental articles of more than 700-h.p.

In power plant evolution, the stagnation pattern so evident in the whole aircraft field existed. Except for racing applications, the maximum power available stayed in the 400- to 500-h.p. range for about ten years, and it was the mid-1930s before 700 + -h.p. was available for service use.

It is not necessary to go back further than the end of World War I to find the origins of the types and missions of aircraft in war, which remained the basis for the military aircraft of World War II. The attack category assumed the close-support, ground-attack role that had been established in World War I. This type had evolved into twin-engine larger planes such as the XA-14 and the A-18 (in production) by 1935, and by 1939 these and the Douglas A-20 were becoming light bombers. As fighters began demonstrating increased capability, they assumed part of the role; for instance, the A-36 was the attack version of the North American P-51 Mustang.

The observation category had been firmly established during World War I when

With excellent streamlining and a 440-h.p. engine, the Curtiss PW-8 of 1923
represented a major advance over World War I aircraft types.

aircraft were truly the eyes of the Army. The tethered observation balloon performed an identical or supplementary function but, because of its vulnerability, had no continuing use. Artillery spotting, photography, and visual reconnaissance became essential functions for Army operations. In the United States, the philosophy of air power as an adjunct of Army ground operations was overpowering until about 1940. This influence demanded the continuing development of types specially adapted to this supporting function. With the growing capabilities of the bombers and fighters, the emergence of offensive doctrine became predominant, and the pure observation function dropped in *relative* importance. Nevertheless, new types appeared right up to the 0-52 in 1940 and 1941. Then, light liaison types and specially equipped combat types such as the photographic fighters picked up the mission.

There were distinct differences in the evolution of Navy types, although in many cases they came in much the same sizes as, and with performance similar to, corresponding Air Corps types. Roughly speaking, naval aircraft types proliferated with the advent of the carriers in the late 1920s. But since the Navy forces were independent mobile units, the functions of scouting and concentrated attack (torpedo planes, for instance) were indispensable and continued to enjoy a higher priority than they did in the Air Corps.

THE DEVELOPMENTAL PROCESS

In trying to determine the initial point in the development of a particular plane or type, it may be convenient to pick a design, a competition specification, a statement of doctrine, or a formal requirements document. Any or all of these may be valid. However, some error creeps in when selection of any one tends to exclude the others. Actually, any significant development is the result of coincidence of many inputs, some of them obscure.

Occasionally, the necessity to provide a specific tactical justification for a program may lead to a definitive statement of purpose. This may be only one possible use and not necessarily the one most likely to be predominant in the future. The justification of the B-17 to reinforce Panama, Alaska, and Hawaii is a case in point.

While operational requirements do *dictate*, the technical capabilities *determine* whether the requirements can be met and what requirements, as yet unstated, may be possible. This essential compromise is always present, and it is wrong to assume that either aspect alone represents the starting point.

Chase, pursuit, fighter, obervation, reconnaissance, scout, light bomber, heavy bomber, attack, patrol, scout bomber, torpedo, tactical, and strategic are terms used to specify types of aircraft. But this is somewhat misleading since the terms define missions or employment. In attempting to follow evolution, perhaps a consideration of size groupings is more revealing.

There is a natural tendency to exploit the characteristics most easily attained with the size of the aircraft. For instance, the small sizes can most easily attain high speed and high rates of climb, and they have superior maneuverability. The larger sizes accommodate heavy loads, alternatively swapping fuel for bombs and vice versa, and need less maneuverability.

It follows that a mission requirement dictates an appropriate size and the characteristics accompanying it. But conversely a given size with suitable characteristics dictates the missions for which it will probably be used. There is a little of both approaches in specifying a specific type. Some confusion arises when the large number of variables relating to "suitable to the size" or "suitable to the mission" are too rigidly fixed. This happens frequently; as a result, many planes are too rigidly designed to a given design point and thus appear to belie a trend or somehow fail to gain acceptability.

Some of the variation of characteristics with size and performance is expressed in the age-old principle of naval surface warfare, "You have to outrun what you can't outgun, and outgun what you can't outrun." Large aircraft are limited in maneuver and dash performance, partly by size, partly by the loss in load-carrying capability when they have enough power to attain high performance, and partly because it is preferable to sacrifice some of the excess structural weight necessary for violent maneuver in favor of additional useful load-carrying capacity. Defense, therefore, indicates defensive armament, defensive formations, and the use of flight paths or night flight to limit or degrade interception.

In the small sizes, maneuver, including dive and climb, becomes defensive as well as offensive. Therefore, it is expected that the armament will be primarily offensive and generally capable of being used on a variety of targets. Tactics will be offensive in that they will try to bring a superior number of the attackers to the target area and then exercise the time-honored principles of surprise and mass.

These factors had been well established by the end of World War I. Fighters, observation types, and light bombers, medium bombers, and a few heavy bombers represented names and functions applied to types as they progressed up the size scale. Of course, there were many missions (for instance, photography and reconnaissance) flown by aircraft that were appropriate to the size or type but did not involve shooting at enemy aircraft or dropping bombs. Particularly later on, up to and including World War II, some of these special uses required specialized arrangements to justify types exclusively for these missions. However, the technical facts of life at any point in history applied as much to specialized cases as to the smaller high-performance planes and the larger load carriers, regardless of the operational uses to which they were put.

THE STATE OF THE ART

The phrase "state of the art" indicates the degree to which evolving design and construction techniques are applied. Although this includes aerodynamics, power plants, fuel, structures, and equipment, the basic elements of the airplane are the wing and the power plant. It follows that as the efficiency of the wing and the power plant improves, so does the performance and the operational capability. In order to follow the evolution of military types during the period between 1927 and 1940, it is essential to evaluate more than the specification data of a series of individual planes; the state of the art applicable to all can be expressed in a variety of applications. For instance, a souped-up racer demonstrates a *potential* that could be realized sometime soon in operational types, and a large civil transport indicates design and construction capabilities that could be applied to military bombers.

The efficiency of the wing is shown in its ability to develop lift compared to its drag, or resistance, which determines the power to move it through the air. This ratio of lift to drag, L/D, varies throughout the flight range from minimum speed to high. As would have been expected, research strove to improve this characteristic, and succeeded.

Power plant efficiency depends both upon the weight of the engine compared to the power it produces and upon the efficiency with which it burns fuel—the pounds/horsepower and the specific fuel consumption, pounds-of-fuel/horsepower/unit-time. These power factors determine the percentage of the total lifting capability of the wing that must be allocated to dragging the plane through the air. Since at a given speed the wing develops a finite total lift, any savings in power plant and fuel weight can be applied directly to useful load. Consequently, research strove to

The Fokker D. VII was a superlative German World War I fighter that featured a steel-tube fuselage and an advanced wing.

improve these efficiency ratios, and it did.

But the lift and drag of complete airplanes is a function of more than the value of the individual elements determined by research testing on component test specimens. Early airplanes used wire bracing and awkward trussing to obtain the structural strength necessary to support the plane and provide added strength for maneuvering flight. The struts and wires offered resistance, or drag, which had to be overcome by power but provided no benefits to the L/D of the complete airplane.

The externally braced biplane of World War I remained in general use through the early 1930s. This type was further degraded by the interference of the struts and wire with the airflow over the wing and the influence of one wing on the other. A notable exception was the Fokker D. VII.

At a meetng at MIT in 1928, Anthony Fokker said that in designing the D. VII he used a biplane arrangement, but the wings were cantilevered without external wires. In the triplane that preceded this type, he had designed the wings to be fully cantilevered without struts or wires. The unconventional appearance led the German authorities to insist on some concessions to conventionality, so he included the interplane struts for cosmetic reasons. Since struts were apparently desirable, he used them with the D. VII to transfer the torsional or twisting loads for one wing to the other. He expressed his horror at visiting a test station and seeing the testing agency about to fly the D. VII with struts removed, having now accepted the possibility that wing strength could be obtained internally. By strenuous argument, he convinced them that the struts in this case were necessary to avoid almost certain risk of flutter and destruction.

Monoplanes, whether wire- or strut-braced, were flown from the very earliest days of human flight. A few examples existed at the end of World War I—including the Bristol Bullet, the Morane Saulnier, which might have superseded the biplanes. 75

Known as the Peashooter, the Boeing P-26 was the first monoplane fighter produced for the Army. It retained such biplane features as an open cockpit, fixed landing gear, and wire-braced wings.

In the mid-1930s, this externally braced monoplane was the model for several types of American military aircraft: the P-26, A-8, A-12, O-35, and B-7, to name some.

Racing planes (notably, the Supermarine S-6, the Gee Bee, and the Travel Air Mystery plane) also used this configuration. But the externally braced monoplane was a transitional form. This was partly the result of the use of relatively thin wings that did not provide enough depth to develop adequate strength in their internal structure. It was also caused by inherited structural concepts that used wooden spars of uniform depth along the span with wire bracing for fore and aft loads in the plane of the wing and then covered the whole wing with fabric.

Although the Junkers all-metal, cantilever monoplane had appeared by 1919, it was not until the late 1920s, when aerodynamic improvements and structural developments using stressed skins came into general use, that the external bracing was eliminated. Here again, one finds the influence of civilian design upon military applications, since most of the new, large transports were cantilever monoplanes.

Basic design concepts for military aircraft did not change materially from the end of World War I until about 1927–30. This artificial stagnation in the military was partly due to the presence in the inventory of earlier obsolete types. Although some new types had come into being, only a few planes had actually been built. The

Know as the "Iron Donkey," the Junkers D.I of 1917 was the first operational all-metal fighter.

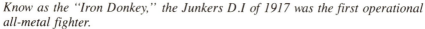

Both rugged and fast, the SPAD XIII equipped more squadrons of the American Expeditionary Forces in France than any other World War I fighter.

appearance of the B-10 in 1934 marked a significant change in performance, configuration, and quantity. But except for this aircraft, the element of innovation that accompanies high rates of production in a substantial industry was lacking.

Pictures of representative planes from the end of World War I through the 1920s reveal that their appearances did not change very much, even though there may have been some improvements in aerodynamics and structure. Representative articles might be the Fokker D. VII, SPAD XIII, SE-5, MB-3, PW-1, P-1, P-12 as fighters; the D.H.4, 0-1, 0-2, 0-19 as middle-sized observation types; and the Handley-Page, Martin, Curtiss B-2, Keystone B-3 as bombers.

PROCUREMENT POLICIES

Procurement policies affected the pattern of evolution in strange ways. An initial procurement, even of an experimental article, gave the government the design rights. A controversial policy permitted the government to go out on competitive bids for subsequent articles. Frequently, the quantity order went to a company other than the original designer or producer. This could set up a competitor in new line, and the risk of this occurring added an element of reluctance to submit new designs or products.

For instance, Curtiss built Martin Bombers and Orenco Model D fighters, which put Martin out of the bomber business for a while and Orenco out of business completely. Thomas Morse developed the MB-3 and built 60, but Boeing got the order for 200. Incidentally, this 200-plane order was the largest quantity of any aircraft type procured between 1922 and 1939, when some 500 P-40s were procured in a series of orders, stimulated by the rising threat of war. After having gotten into the bomber business with the Martin production Curtiss followed with its own B-2, and Martin went into predominantly Navy business for a few years. Boeing, having built the MB-3s, was able to compete successfully, with the PW-9 taking over from the Curtiss PW-8, which had itself been an outgrowth of the Curtiss racing planes. Curtiss countered with a modification of the PW-8, using a tapered wing as Boeing had done in the PW-9; this became the P-1 Hawk, which, in series evolution, lasted through the P-6 in 1934 and ended with a single experimental version, the YP-23.

Immediately after World War I, there were a number of efforts to convert or modify late military types to civilian use. Martin made a transport version and a

Initially designated P-16, twenty-six Berliner-Joyce PB-1 two-seat fighters were built in 1929.

mail version of its bomber. The Dayton Wright Company converted D.H.4s to passenger use by adding enclosures over the rear cockpit. England had several versions of bombers adapted to passenger service. Fokker even made a modification of the D. VII with a small cabin behind the pilot, which was entered by a side door. In America, the only successful alterations of this sort were the passenger cabin arrangements of the naval patrol boats that saw some extended service and helped to inaugurate some of our first regular airline service.

While it is easy to appreciate the transfer of basic technology back and forth from civilian to military applications, there were always a few cases where complete articles provided mutual support. In 1929, Curtiss built a passenger cabin version of the B-2 called the Condor. This went on to become the familiar Condor transport used by the airlines until about 1935. Although the new plane was quite different from the bomber, its origin was clear. In the 1935 transport competition, which Douglas won with the C-33, a cargo-door version of the DC-2, Curtiss submitted a cargo version of the commercial Condor. What had started from the experience with the Martin Bomber evolved over a period of twelve or thirteen years into a craft that met the current military requirements and might have come back into the inventory as a transport. Later examples included the B-18, which was a military version of the DC-2; the Boeing Stratoliner, which was a transport take-off from the B-17; and the big Boeing 314 Clipper flying boat used by Pan American, which had developed from the B-15.

It is popular to select individual aircraft types and trace their evolution through their various models. This is perfectly valid but unnecessary in summarizing trends. Detailed descriptions and specifications are contained in many excellent references. These may be used to illustrate trends that are in reality based on more generalized data.

A COMBINATION OF DISCIPLINES

So far, the considerations have been devoted to missions and sizes of aircraft resulting in configurations and performance characteristics of complete aircraft. But the complete weapon system brings together a complex variety of technical disciplines, each of which has its own limitations, capabilities, and concepts. The use of available materials and technologies determines the performance quality of a design initiated as of any one date. The application and combination of all these elements that are available at any particular time is the state of the art. Since these elements are continually being altered by basic research and increasing knowledge, a few month's difference in the starting date of a project can make a significant difference in the quality, the size, and eventually the looks of the resulting design, allowing for differences in design capability.

The availability of a new alloy or the development of a technique for working it may permit allocating less weight to structure. A new model engine or a development in cooling technique will change the attainable performance. Each technical area deserves considerable elaboration though it would be interesting primarily to the specialist. Nevertheless, the characteristics and performances of these emerging types cannot be appreciated without considering the impact of these component factors.

In tracing the origins of the specific types that comprised the wartime force, one finds that the impact of these technical inputs was more important to the force as a whole than to the configuration and arrangement. For instance, the laminar-flow wing section, developed by Eastman Jacobs at NACA, became available in 1938 and 1939 as the P-51 design was being started and was included in the new aircraft. This one element accounted for some of the superior performance of this plane in combat.

Only one Barling NBL-1 was built (in 1923), and its outdated performance precluded further orders for the type.

Distinguished for being the first pressurized, four-engine airliner built in the United States, the Boeing Model 307 Stratoliner was a success, in part because of its use of the Boeing B-17 wings and tail.

79

Because these factors change continuously and at differing times, it is difficult to determine the exact point at which they combine with operational doctrine and procurement programs. There are basic design considerations and compromises that are fundamental to all airplane design and finally determine the configuration, size, and performance regardless of the time period or the state of the art. A summary of these seems dull to the nontechnical individual and too simple to the engineer, but it does serve to help one appreciate the underlying source of the quality of any particular type.

One of the first considerations is the determination of the minimum landing and takeoff speeds. This is an operational factor related to the size and surface of contemplated landing fields. In the mid 1930s, most fields were grass surface, and doctrine dictated the probability of using dispersed and unprepared landing grounds. By 1940, hard-surface runways were in general use. This permitted higher landing speeds and longer takeoff runs and was a significant factor in the improvement in overall performance of planes coming out after 1935.

The minimum speed for landing came from the size (area) of the wing, the characteristics of the wing section used, and the weight. As the minimum acceptable speed increased, either the size could be decreased or the weight for the size could increase. The increasing weight was the most noticeable result. But takeoff, climb, and ceiling required excess power at the high lift angles of the wing, so that power increases had to accompany the higher loads or reductions in size.

This relationship of weight to size is known as "wing loading"—that is, the weight divided by the wing area. It comes out as a figure of pounds per square foot. Not only is the figure a fundamental value in assessing the characteristics or quality of any design, but the trends over time represent overall progress. For instance, at the end of World War I most craft fell in a range of eight to ten pounds per square foot of wing area. By 1930, this range had increased to about twelve to fifteen; by 1935 or 1936, the figures would have been about twenty-five to thirty; and by 1940, the peak was just over forty with the P-38.

It would be misleading to assume that, since the weight that any size could carry increased dramatically over the years, this was all aerodynamic and structural improvement. Even allowing for higher acceptable minimum speeds, the power available had to increase to match the increases in weight just to hold the power loading (weight divided by power) constant. Actually, the relationship between wing

In the early 1930s, seven Douglas Y1B-7s were constructed using advanced concepts such as all-metal skin and retractable landing gear.

loading and power loading demanded that as the wing loading went up, the power loading should come down to provide satisfactory performance and take full advantage of the increased speed and load-carrying potential.

This interrelationship gave rise to many conflicting contentions. The power plant and propulsion people claimed with reasonable justification that performance improvements in the mid-1930s period of drastic change resulted from the power side of the relationship. On the other hand, the airframe designers and builders claimed that most of the improvements came from aerodynamics and structures. Obviously, the external forms of the emerging planes were changing drastically, so the credit cannot go to power alone.

Trying to make tables and lists of wing areas, wing loadings, and power loadings for all types of aircraft would be too overwhelming in technical detail, even though the results would be quite revealing for analytical study. However, any serious record of one type of plane and its subsequent model evolution should include these basic approaches to determine how it compares with others.

Wheel brakes seem incidental as a safety feature or convenience for ground handling. But they permitted shortening ground rolls on landing and thus higher landing speeds and larger weights. By 1930, most planes had been equipped with brakes. Still, there were a number of unbraked planes flying in 1932, and the transition was more involved than would have been expected.

The aircraft that were put into mass production and that became the combat types all had retractable landing gears. This feature was standard by the time the World War II types were in production, but it had only just made the team by about 1935.

From the earliest days of flight, there had been concern over landing gear. There were skids, wheels for takeoff dropped for landing on skids, and varieties of wheeled gears.

In the United States, J.V. Martin claimed the first mechanically operated retractable gear in his Kitten, which is on exhibit in the National Air and Space Museum. This claim was always contested, and there may have been some experimental ventures elsewhere in the world. The Verville-Sperry (Lawrence Sperry) racer of 1922 was a low-wing monoplane with such a gear. The monoplane civil transports such as the Boeing 247 and the Douglas DC-2 used the gear. In the military, the emerging bomber types (B-7, B-9, and B-10) included retractable gear by about 1932. Most of the biplanes except for some like the Grumman F3F and some later

Although advanced for its day, the Northrop A-17 of 1935 was built in relatively small numbers.

Curtiss Hawks stayed with fixed gears. Some went from fixed to retractable as model changes. For instance, the Northrop A-17 was fixed, and the A-17A was retractable. By about 1937, retractable gears were practically universal, although there had been prolonged objections, largely on the grounds of maintenance, complexity, and weight. The last objections were overcome by stressing the safety of emergency belly landings instead of depending on turnover protection to save the crew of low-wing monoplanes in nose-over accidents. It is not possible to trace directly the introdution of an item that was finally accepted as standard and that added so much to performance. Nor is it a simple matter to describe all the different variants. But it is worth noting that it took about fifteen years after the first clear demonstrations to gain acceptance.

The contribution of the tricycle landing gear to the performance of the combat types was very real but not quite as obvious as the drag reduction obtained by pulling the gear inside the aerodynamic shape. Essentially, the tricycle gear's stability on the ground made ground handling, landing, and taking off with heavy and fast airplanes much easier and less tricky. In other words, the newly trained pilots could match performances that formerly required high skills and considerable experience. Translated into performance, the higher gross weights and higher landing speeds could now be used without making allowance for the probable slip in pilot skills in wartime training programs.

By the time mass production of military aircraft started around 1939, tricycle gears were not universal, but a start had been made at introducing them. The designs that originated between 1935 and 1936 were largely committed to configurations using conventional gears. The high-powered single-engine fighters with big propellers would have required long landing-gear legs, which would have been difficult to retract into the small, dense structures. During that critical starting period, there was serious objection from some operational quarters, which made it difficult to specify the tricycles. The experimental nature of the XP-39 permitted specification of the gear, and this was effectively included when introduced early enough.

It is easy to identify the point at which the tricycle gear entered the Air Corps. This was on the experimental installation on the Douglas OA-4 amphibian. About 1936, Carl Greene, at the time head of the Project Officer Section at Wright Field, undertook a study of unconventional landing gear arrangements for heavy aircraft. He was convinced that the tricycle arrangement with a swiveling nose wheel was worth investigating. He managed to start a project that resulted in a contract to Douglas to mount an adjustable system on the amphibian. Curtiss had a tricycle arrangement on the 1910 pusher, but the nose wheel was nonswiveling. In the mid 1930s, Fred Weick at NACA had mounted such a gear on a light airplane. Carl Cover of Douglas and test pilots and project officers from Wright Field evaluated it, and their reports were enthusiastically favorable. In January, 1937, the plane was sent to operating units for a limited service evaluation. The reports from the service were not favorable, so it was not possible to specify it in procurement documents. Except for purely experimental projects where it could be "required," it could only be listed as "acceptable." "How do you stop if you have lost the brakes?" was the most frequent question. Leonard Harman, the bomber project officer suggested, tongue in cheek, that sand pits could be dug at the ends of runways. In any event, the gears became standard because of their obvious advantages, but it took time.

The one component development that was probably most significant in the improvement in performance and that was available to all applications was the almost universal use of *wing flaps*. From the earliest days of flight, there were ideas of varying wing area, or the curvature of the wing. In the mid-1920s, the trailing edge flap and the Handley Page leading edge slot began to appear. The Guggenheim

Safe Airplane Competition in 1929 specified such difficult low-speed performance that there were a number of variations of these devices aimed primarily at improving the low-speed, landing, and take-off performances. The new transports in the early 1930s included flaps, but the military types, even the low-wing monoplane configurations, did not include them in the first generations.

By depressing a wing's trailing edge, wing flaps increase the downwash as the air leaves the wing and thereby increase the lift reaction. The flaps also increase the drag, which makes for steeper gliding approaches. The earlier biplanes had so much drag that the approaches were steep enough; when pulled up to high angles for landing, the planes settled quickly and slowed down in the ground roll.

The clean monoplanes came in faster and flatter without flaps. Small changes in dive angle caused large variations in approach speed and tendency for the plane to float close to the ground, making accurate landings difficult. To obtain the best landing distance with the first of these clean, unflapped planes required that approaches be flown close to the stall, perhaps as little as three miles per hour above the stalling speed. This gave only one chance for a quick flare at ground level.

Some versions of flaps extended to the rear beyond the trailing edge of the wing. This arrangement both increased wing area and changed the curvature. The combination further reduced the stalling speed and, as a bonus, permitted partial extension to improve takeoff.

The wing flap was one of the few improvements that provided desirable technical and operational benefits with its introduction without creating new problems. This may have accounted for its relatively rapid acceptance, so that it was standard by about 1935.

Flaps had both immediate and secondary effects. They reduced the stalling or landing speed by ten to twenty miles per hour and shortened landing and takeoff ground run by about 20 percent. This was a major factor in permitting the load-carrying ability (wing loading) to increase. As a result, the plane size could be smaller for any planned gross weight, resulting in less drag, which in turn provided substantial benefits in high speed.

Today, these elements are commonly available and included, at least to some degree, in almost all aircraft. They tend to be taken for granted and neglected in assessing credit for performance. But forty years ago, they were the key to the overall performance of the entire American force and served to maintain parity with foreign competition.

These elements need not be traced, except by technicians interested in individual specialities. It is helpful, however, to list some to indicate the scope. They include structural concepts, materials, fuels, power plant developments, and instruments. Two that deserve elaboration are propellers and superchargers.

PROPELLERS

Early propellers were wooden and were designed with a compromise diameter and pitch. The diameter was selected to match, or suit, the rotational speed of the engine with some assumed speed of the airplane. This selection was to keep the combined forward speed and rotational speed of the tips below the speed of sound or in an efficient range. The pitch was selected to favor either high speed or takeoff and climb. These selections were modified by the altitude range in which it was hoped to fly.

The blade settings were obviously fixed during the manufacture of the one-piece propeller. Consequently, if the property was good in one part of the operating range, it was relatively inefficient at the other end. If selected for an intermediate performance, both ends of the spectrum—speed on the one hand, climb on the other—were degraded. If some mismatch occurred or a different performance range was desired, the only remedy was to make a new propeller.

Then in the early 1920s, metal and other materials began to be used for blades. The next step in the mid-1920s was the separate hub with demountable blades. This permitted ground adjustment of the blades.

About 1928, Frank Caldwell, working for the Hamilton Standard Company, invented the two-position controllable hub. This permitted a high-pitch and a low-pitch blade angle to be selected by the pilot in flight. This form was in production by 1932 and was immediately adopted by the airlines and the military. In 1933, Hamilton Standard and Caldwell received the Collier Trophy from President Roosevelt for their achievement.

By 1934, Caldwell and company had devised a governor control that enabled the pilot to select a desired speed (rpm), which was then automatically held constant by the propeller mechanism. This permitted continuous automatic pitch adjustment that could more nearly approach the most efficient pitch setting for all regimes of flight.

The constant-speed propeller was the big break in propulsion. It was a necessary companion to flaps, which provided the aerodynamic capability of increasing the range of speed from minimum to high. As power plant development improved performances at high altitudes with supercharging, the constant-speed propeller also provided the pitch adjustment necessary to accommodate changing altitude.

By about 1938, the full-feathering propeller came in to extend the capability of the constant-speed hub. This development was essential for multi-engine heavy airplanes. If the blades were twisted into a nearly fore-and-aft alignment, they stopped rotating. With the blades lined up with the wind, the drag was greatly reduced with a dead engine so that the remaining engine or engines stood a better chance of keeping the plane aloft and up to speed.

There were other approaches to the constant-speed principle. Curtiss, which used electric mechanisms instead of the hydraulic ones of Hamilton Standard, was a major supplier. Curtiss used steel blades, and Hamilton Standard aluminum. Different materials and different systems amounted to more than competition. In an emergency, additional manufacturers permitted tapping a broader source of suppliers.

The advantages for heavy airplanes, principally for takeoff, climb, and maximum cruise, are obvious. For maneuvering fighters, constant-speed propellers were equally effective because the planes' speeds and altitudes change continually and because variable power management is an essential part of combat. In the case of the very large airplanes—for instance, XB-15 and XB-19—the availability of constant-speed propellers in 1935 was significant. Having the propellers may not have been a decisive element in the initiation of the projects, but it made the programs feasible.

In the 1920s, a D.H.4 with a supercharger and wooden fixed-pitch propeller illustrated the engineering-piloting problem. The propeller was about two feet in diameter larger than normal to absorb the power at very high altitude. This required a greatly extended landing gear to keep the propeller tips off the ground. To match the speed at high altitude, the blades had a steep pitch and were quite wide. For takeoff and flying at low speed and altitude, the big prop kept the engine from turning up to full power. Furthermore, the blade angle was so steep that it was practically stalled with very little thrust. With the power held way down by the big props and the efficiency kept very low, the acceleration was sluggish; the plane needed a big field to get off, and the climb was awful. But it made a good photographic plant at high altitude. The turbosupercharger maintained full power at full rpm up to about 20,000 feet, but this altitude capability exaggerated the propeller problem.

The timing was fortunate. The availability of the constant-speed propeller in 1935 occurred in time to be included in the initial design concepts of the aircraft that became the seed stock for the expansion four years later. By comparison, some European aircraft were using fixed-pitch wooden propellers at the opening of hostilities. By having propellers that could accommodate the rapidly increasing availability of altitude power from engine development, improved performance could be cranked in even before expanded production reached full swing.

SUPERCHARGERS

Airplane engines have always struggled to get better altitude performance. The engine, being just an air pump, gasps for air at the rarefied altitudes and has difficulty cramming in sufficient oxygen to burn enough fuel to develop power.

There are several approaches. One is to make a larger engine than necessary and keep it partly throttled at low altitude, opening it up to full pumping capacity as higher altitude is reached. Supplementary pumps can be added to compress air before it enters the combustion chambers. Root's blowers, the big dumbbell-shaped pumps with two-lobe gears that intermesh to move large volumes of air much as a geared oil pump moves fluid, have been used.These are mechanically driven from the power section. More common are centrifugal blowers, either shaft-driven or driven by exhaust turbines run by exhaust gas.

It is not necessary to pinpoint the evolution of each form with each engine maker to establish that the supercharging available for the war effort was about twenty years in coming. If the critical altitudes at which the engines maintained their power are simply listed, it is seen that the progress had been impressive. In speed alone, which gained about 1 percent per thousand-foot increase in altitude, the impact of supercharging on the performance of the wartime fleet was obviously considerable. Even more significant was the relative ability of competing forces to attain superior ceiling altitude.This may have been more crucial to survival and victory than was speed.

The turbosupercharger had a profound effect on the performance of American planes. The B-17, B-24, P-38, and P-47 were equipped with them. But if we go back in time, we see that these superchargers gave this country the potential for reaching critical altitudes of 20,000 feet all the way back in the 1920s. Although few series production types were equipped, there were always a few experimental or special mission articles mounting the turbo. This is not meant to slight the increasing supercharging built into the mechanically driven blowers. But in some respects, the existence of the turbo paced the drive to get even higher altitude performance.

Aside from the aircraft used in combat, some of the others were the P-43, P-37, FM-1, PB-2A, P-23, D.H.4, Martin Bomber of 1922, and Packard Lepère of 1919. Maj. Rudolph Schroeder established a world's altitude record of 33,133 feet with the Lepère in 1920, and Lt. J. A. Macready reached 40,800 feet with it in 1921.

The turbo first appeared in France in 1916, and the data on it were furnished to the United States upon our entry into World War I. General Electric was selected to develop it, and Dr. Sanford Moss was in charge of the effort. It was tested with a 350-h.p. Liberty engine high on Pike's Peak, delivering slightly more than sea-level power at about 14,000 feet.

The end of the war cancelled the project, but it was reinstated in 1919. So there is a continuous record from this early date all the way to the B-29s that ended World War II and substantially marked the end of reciprocating engines in military planes. 85

MODEL CHANGES

All the detailed summaries of individual type characteristics reveal a large number of model changes and, with some changes in power plants, type number changes as well. This was in large measure the result of limited procurement. To keep abreast of advances in the state of the art, a given initial procurement was extended by modification as far as possible. An outstanding example was the B-23. The original DB-1 prototype by Douglas was a bomber adaptation of the DC-2. Procured as the B-18, it went through a further modification as the B-18A, which corresponded to the DC-3. In an effort to develop an advanced version using the R-2600 engines and a redesigned fuselage giving more performance, the last thirty articles were change-ordered to B-23s.

By stretching out the delivery, it was hoped a reorder capability could be retained against the possibility that quantities might be needed. The reorder possibility ran out before funds became available, so a bomber that was as good as any in the world in the early stages of the war died without quantity production.

Although no doctrine existed for planned model changes, a sort of tacit philosophy seemed to combine the change-order procurement with state of the art progress to produce a casual pattern.

A graph of performance versus time can help indicate a general principle. "Performance" can be the change with time of either a single element such as speed, or a concept such as overall performance suitable for the category being considered, or a number of qualities (e.g., load, range, ceiling, speed).

Any initial article existing at a time can be *X-1*, a successful experimental type representative of various individual solutions of the same time period and with performance falling near the representative performance line.

As subsequent advances in the state of the art permit, it will be advantageous to produce new model variations. A service test version *Y* will be followed by series production on model changes *A, B, C,* etc. The average slope of progress is determined more nearly by the initial improvements that can be cranked into existing models, as indicated by *Y* and *A*, than by the bold ventures.

The Curtiss YA-8 was developed as a two-seat ground attack aircraft in 1930. Though a modern all-metal military monoplane, it nevertheless featured wire-braced wings.

The Curtiss YP-37 featured a liquid-cooled power plant. Thirteen of these aircraft were built.

However, after some steps are taken, basic configuration and structural practices limit the advances that can be made, and the models *B* and *C* drift below the line. Then, completely new types have to be projected. But here it is not enóugh to project along the extended line. It must be expected that there will be time slippages or real deficiencies below the hoped-for performance, so an advanced position such as *X-2* is taken. If the time delays are serious or the performance is difficult to attain, the experimental project may in reality drift.

During the 1930s, similarly planned model improvements had to be evaluated by being projected laterally in time to the date when quantities could be made available. Consequently, many diverse models, though they represented potential performance that could have provided some insurance, never made it into the American military inventory. Some experimental articles still suffer the same fate, even though they do establish the practicality of reducing advanced ideas to practice. Procurement policies and funding affect the possibility of introducing desirable models and force the procurement of less than desirable forms.

It was apparent all through the 1930s that one desirable format was to have at all times in each combat cateogry one experimental article, a limited number of service test articles from which to pick the next generation of production, and ongoing production that could be amplified as needed. Since each combat category needed this approach, it could never be achieved with limited funding. But as an informal guide, the plan was extremely valuable because it paced gaps in production and set standards for future developemnts.

HIGHER SPEEDS

So it was that design studies in 1935 and 1936 indicated that after 1940 fighters should have high speeds of over 400 mph, with operating altitudes of 20,000 feet and better, and should carry armament loads roughly four times the current standard loads. Bombers by the same criteria should have speeds roughly twice their current capabilities, operate at 20,000 feet and better, and carry loads two to four times current practice, with range roughly twice the current distance. This translated into machines about four times the size and weight of those in existence. To power these advanced types, power plants would have to be in the 2,000-h.p. range, with four engines instead of the conventional two.

With the shortage of funds, the small size of the industry, and the apathy of the country, this seemed well nigh impossible. Competition was not limited to company versus company, or Army versus Navy, or any other domestic consideration. Enemy potential had to be considered, too. Since it had to be assumed that any foreign power could use the same state of the art, the potential improvement in possible enemy performance was a real factor, which made the demands very real and most urgent. The engineering figures represented the opposite side of the same coin, describing the tactical desires of the operating units and planners. A cliché form of the operating requirement was "10,000 pounds of bombs carried 10,000 miles."

If speed is taken as a single characteristic representing overall performance, then an appreciation of the advances in technology can be easily summarized. The ratio of maximum speed to minimum speed is a simple indicator. It represents the performance corresponding to maximum lift compared to the minimum drag of the complete aircraft as attainable with the available total power plant efficiency.

At the end of World War I, this speed ratio was approximately two to one. At the end of the biplane era in the early 1930s, this ratio was about two and one-half to one. And in the mid-1930s, the first of the cantilever monoplane fighters, which were designed for maximum speed, achieved ratios of about three to one. But by World War II even with the first production articles, the speed range was over four. Some of this was due to higher critical altitudes of the engines, since speed increases about 1 percent with each 1,000 feet of increased altitude at the same power. This altitude power factor accounts for only about 10 percent of the total gain. Perhaps better than any other summary, the doubling of the speed ratio indicates the continued development of applied technology, even in spite of limited development funds and limited procurement. An example of differences of opinion lies in power plant protagonists' claim that 70 percent of the improvement was due to engines. It all depends on the assumptions, but both factors were present.

WING LOADING

It is easy to say that wing loading increased from about seven to ten pounds per square foot in the early 1920s to about fifty to sixty pounds per square foot in the early 1940s. But this is only part of the story. When the loading increase is greater than the aerodynamic lift of the wing, a higher minimum speed results. This translates into longer takeoffs and landings at higher speeds. But since the lifting power of the actual wing on the airplane gets its lift from the square power of the speed, small increases in speed compensate by providing considerable increase in lift. So although fields were increased in length and hard-surfaced runways were substituted for grass fields, by far the greatest portion of the advance came from improved aerodynamics and power plants, aided by high lift devices such as flaps and slots, that were employed only in the maximum lift condition.

WEIGHTS

Weight, all-up gross weight, has long been used to describe how big an airplane is. It is evident from the changes in wing loading over the years that weights are a very imperfect measure of size. This is particularly difficult when comparing different generations separated by a few years. Some geometric dimension like wing span might be used, but since the wing *area* is the fundamental characteristic of an airplane to which all other charactristics relate, some interesting conclusions may be drawn by using this dimension as the entering point for examining progress.

If there were some standard wing areas established for certain combat functions that pertained over an extended period, similar to the standard gauge rail and wheel

When it was introduced, the Boeing B-9 bomber could outrun any fighter in the Air Corps.

tread devised for surface vehicles, wing loading would be an accurate measure of progress, and all variations from a mean line would explain measured deviations in performance or maneuver characteristics. In the days when getting into the air any way at all was an accomplishment, it was assumed that an airplane could only perform one specific function for which it had been designed. However, the plane itself was always able to do anything that fell within its performance and maneuverability envelope.

SPECIFIC DESIGN

In spite of the inherent flexibility of aerial employment, specific characteristics have always dictated design with a corresponding impact on size. Consquently, it is impossible to find coincidence of size and mission except where large numbers of types happen to exist for similar purposes. This occurs in both military and civilian aviation. In the military particularly, it is almost axiomatic that weapons created for a specific purpose are used for purposes not even visualized when the initial design was contemplated. Even in civilian applications where detailed market surveys indicate certain sizes or features, time changes need, and the airplane is used for a variety of missions over a long life span.

How deeply ingrained this concept of specific design is can be illustrated by a meeting with de Havilland engineers during World War II. When it was suggested that the flexibility of an aircraft required early consideration of its potential for numerous duties and that its performance characteristics as well as its provisions for special mission equipment should be balanced with this in mind (even when the initial requirement did not contemplate such uses), there was an immediate outcry. The engineers maintained that such considerations would unduly degrade the machine. When asked how many versions of the Mosquito were being built, they replied twelve or thirteen. The Mosquito was a superb aircraft, used efficiently for many missions, but even the engineers building the plane thought that they were building single-purpose articles. In reality, the only differences were in equipment carried and in the training of crew members.

While a hypothetical progression of sizes with discreet intervals can be postulated, the scattering of sizes and types in different time periods confuses the issue. However, considering the smallest combat type, the fighter, with the simplest 89

The British S.E.5a was one of the best World War I fighters. It was adopted by the U.S. Army Air Service after the war.

requirement for performance, maneuvering, and armament, an interesting and revealing coincidence appears.

The Deperdussin of 1913 was the first really high-speed or high-performance airplane. It had a wing area of about 225 square feet. World War I fighters—the SE-5, SPAD, Fokker D. VII— had wing areas varying from 211 to 240 square feet. The postwar biplane fighters had wing areas of about 250 square feet. The monoplanes of the late 1930s—except for special cases represented by the P-38 and P-47—were very close to 235 square feet. Considering that they represented the products of widely diversified design teams and stemmed from different requirement inputs, there is a remarkable uniformity.

It appears that a wing area of 235 square feet has been correct for traditional-sized fighters at least as far back as World War I. Perhaps fighter pilots are really conservative and traditional types in spite of dramatic presentations to the contrary. In 1934, a survey was submitted to all fighter units requesting guidance in specifying the characteristics for follow-on types to replace the P-12s. After considerable effort on the part of the operating units, the replies indicated that what was wanted was a plane like the P-12, except faster.

Designers committed to one category—bombers, for instance—may be so involved with the considerations for that one type that they miss the opportunity to compete for some other type. Some oufits specialize in certain types but are forced, under the pressures of survival, to move into other fields. This may just force them out of step with a procurement pattern or with evolution into another field.

ABILITY TO PRODUCE

Underlying all other considerations is a factor called "ability to produce." This applies particularly in periods of scarcity. An existing facility having plant, tools, personnel, and engineering and manufacturing capability represents a national resource worth preserving. It is irresponsible to let this disintegrate in order to follow a "will-o'-the-wisp" proposal that is attractive but has not been reduced to practice. During the time lost in building a new capability from scratch, one of the

Regarded as a classic pursuit ship of the early 1930s, the Boeing P-12 was the last biplane fighter used by the Air Corps.

proven facilities might well achieve the same results promised by the first outfit but without the risks. In retrospect, it is always easy to be critical of decisions or lack of decision about alternatives, when actually there were frequently no practical or legal alternatives available.

Although the ingredients may be obvious, the mix refects the distinctive character of the design and manufacturing team, colored by the economic and management inputs from the customer and producer. To appreciate how these multifaceted factors interact, some specific applications can be followed. All of them stem from distant antecedents, some general and some peculiar, to a particular type or developer. There are no instant marvels.

It is safe to say that the *ability* to recognize need, to design, to fabricate, to test, to develop, and to use always exist, even with a restricted activity. But it is difficult to keep this ability current. It must be assumed, when referring to the whole national potential, that if one approach succeeds others could have, too. Conversely, if one opportunity is lost, another will take its place. Consequently, in evaluating the overall situation, it is better to understand the fundamentals that indicate what could have happened or what was bound to happen. What did happen represents the coincidence of a unique selection of fundamentals. It also represents the equally complex interrelationship of all the factors that make it possible for different weapon systems to appear in usable form at any particular time in history—as at the beginning of World War II.

V THE MILITARY AND THE AIRCRAFT INDUSTRY

When President Eisenhower warned the country against the dangers of a "military-industrial" complex, he could not have been referring to the relationship that existed between the aircraft industry and the armed forces during the period of the 1930s. Whatever it might have been called, that relationship was the principal reason the United States was able to create the air power that became such a potent force for victory in World War II.

If the elements composing the "complex" had been categorized, they might have been separated into three groupings—military, research and education, and civilian aviation. There were army aviators, naval aviators, commercial and private aviators, aircraft manufacturers, engine manufacturers, component and accessories manufacturers, aviation researchers, and general aviation and airlines. No matter their sources of income, the tie that bound them all, individuals and units alike, was an unrelenting faith in the future of flight.

THE AVIATION COMMUNITY

Most professions and industries have always had associations, committees, and professional societies to bring their participants together from time to time. The aircraft industry was no exception during the 1930s. Like other industrial groups, there was the usual exchange of ideas and experiences aimed at furthering the common interest and the level of technology.

Faith inspired a feeling of fighting against odds. Any serious appraisal of the times indicates that the odds were real and not imaginary. First, aviation was still new. Although its existence was recognized, it had not been accepted as a legitimate member of the economic and political family. Secondly, there was little prospect of making a financial killing in the game. If some industrialists had been attracted by the promotional possibilities in 1927, the Depression years had disillusioned them. The group that remained was primarily dedicated to *aviation*, with survival seeming to be a higher priority than profit. Fortunately, many who avoided or survived bankruptcy, or who moved from one organization to another, were financially rewarded. But until about 1938, everyone had a common bond in adversity.

The earliest military aircraft experiences had served to establish a tradition of cooperation that transcended the military/civilian boundaries. The Wright brothers and Glenn H. Curtiss ran schools to train military aviators. The first landing of an airplane on a ship at sea occurred January 18, 1911, some thirteen miles off San Francisco when Eugene Ely, an exhibition pilot, landed and took off from the *Pennsylvania*. The first Wright Army aircraft at Fort Sam Houston was maintained, at least part of the time, with money supplied by the pilots and mechanics until Army appropriations could cover the costs of bamboo, wire, and fabric.

At the conclusion of World War I, a significant number of military aviators, as well as engineers and other civilians who had entered the aviation industry, continued in aeronautical pursuits. There were a number of outstanding military aviators and engineers who had stayed in the service temporarily but then left to go into industry or other civilian aeronautical activities. A stimulus for exodus was slow promotion. A wartime officer might expect to remain a lieutenant for up to seventeen years. Reuben Fleet left to start his own manufacturing company, which eventually became Consolidated Aircraft. Eric Nelson, of the round-the-world flight, went with Boeing. Charles Montieth, an outstanding engineer and author of one of the first definitive books on design, also left to join Boeing. Harry Sutton, a survivor of the early spin testing, became a vice president for Fleet at Consolidated. Carl Cover became a vice president at Douglas. James Doolittle went with Shell Oil, and Edwin Aldrin set up a corresponding aircraft division for Standard Oil and was joined by Will White. Alford Williams, noted for his record-breaking flights in the Navy Curtiss racing planes, gained even more prominence in his activity with Gulf Oil. Though they constitute only a small sampling, these examples indicate the intimacy of the relationship between the military and the industry.

Without resigning, military pilots did have some access across military/civilian boundaries. They took leave to do specific testing or demonstration flights for struggling manufacturers. McCullough performed flight and spin tests for Fleet. While still in the service, Doolittle, Leigh Wade, and Joseph A. Cannon flew Curtiss planes in foreign demonstrations. Stanley M. Ulmstead was one of the test pilots for the Guggenheim Safe Airplane Competition.

The large block of regular officers remaining from World War I formed a bulge in the promotion lists that used up most of the allocated spaces up to about 1930. The graduates of the military academies were assured regular commissions, so many of the newly trained aviators received reserve commissions and served for limited periods of active duty. Returning to inactive status, they frequently took jobs with the expanding airlines, with manufacturers, or in other slots in civilian aviation. They retained a bilateral relationship with civilian aviation and military aviation. An outstanding example was Charles Lindbergh.

During the 1930s, a somewhat different relationship developed. But it, too, served to retain a close contact and an interchange of ideas. Contractors or manufacturers made a practice of demonstrating their aircraft to the military even though there was little or no chance of military procurement. To a varying degree, the military in return offered comments on design and flight characteristics. Since most companies were building both civilian and military planes, there was considerable interchange of design and manufacturing concepts both inside the plants and between military and civilian organizations.

As an example, after Douglas completed the first DC-4, which eventually went to Japan, in 1938, Carl Cover brought it to Wright Field to be examined by engineers and flight crews. He provided a number of demonstration flights at the time, and later both the bomber and fighter project officers were permitted to fly it at the factory. Incidentally, Orville Wright was a passenger on one of the flights at Wright Field.

One other factor provided cement for the "complex" that facilitated progress. During the 1920s and early 1930s, few colleges offered aeronautical engineering courses; the Guggenheim Fund did much to increase the availability of this training. The military regularly sent outstanding aviators to these schools for graduate training.

The result of this concentration of training was that military personnel came to know many students and faculty members and vice versa. Furthermore, the students who graduated to civilian jobs in the industry or research had established lasting bonds of friendship that bridged the gaps of organizational affiliation.

MILITARY/CIVILIAN RELATIONSHIPS

The essence of the situation, prior to the buildup that occurred about 1939, was that since there were so few people involved, direct communication and mutual trust were normal and instinctive. The investigative reporter of the 1960–70 period would have been appalled by the lack of formality and by the opportunity for collusion. Although final results were meticulously documented, much of the preliminary negotiation was never recorded.

Aircraft going into service always develop "bugs," those nasty little revelations of unexpected shortcomings. They were inevitable with new materials, new structural concepts, new equipment installations, a new order of performance, and, in some cases, operational employment different than what had been visualized at the outset. The manufacturer's service representatives became almost part of the military organization's maintenance team. They were invaluable both to the service at all technical and procurement levels and to the manufacturers. They channeled operational doctrine back to their organizations, and their service modifications helped provide new standards for the procurement agencies.

For a time, Curtiss made a practice of sending out the project engineer of a new type of aircraft with the first planes going into service. He not only learned the problems of the operating environment but also could solve problems on the spot, which shortened correction times. On his return, he was better able to interpret military requirements in the next generation.

Another factor that shortened the time for industry-wide adoption of innovations was the cross-licensing arrangement for patents conducted through the Manufacturers Aircraft Association, which had been formed in 1917 to expedite the wartime manufacture of airplanes. This system eliminated the conflict of proprietary interests that had handicapped the initial production efforts. The old Wright versus Curtiss struggle and the subsequent difficulties with the J. V. Martin patents illustrate some of the problems. In 1928, civilian production was included in the agreement.

Investigations after World War I proved that the arrangement did not violate antitrust restrictions and had in fact expedited production and cut costs. The industry had a long experience in working together. Although competition was recognized, some of the expensive and time-consuming conflicts were handled by rules of compensation, which set a pattern for mutual trust.

In 1928, before the amended agreement was adopted, there were seventeen members left in the association; a number of wartime manufacturers had ceased to build aircraft for the government. The next year, there were forty-six members, including many companies such as Cessna, Spartan, and others that primarily built small commercial planes but whose activities stimulated aviation in the broader sense.

One of the more subtle influences was the effect of the Reserve Officers Training Corps (ROTC), as the number of colleges offering aeronautics courses increased. A portion of the students joined the Air ROTC or its Navy equivalent. After they were graduated, these students entered the reserves. Some went on active duty, but many went into aviation or related industries. On the other hand, engineering students in other technical fields frequently joined the Air ROTC because of their interest in aviation and preferred to consider service in the air arms in the event of an emergency.

The reserve units, or cadres, in the 1920s were largely made up of persons who had left wartime active service and returned to other business pursuits. This mix of experience shifted as ROTC graduates increased. While it is probably impossible to document, a fair assumption is that in the civilian aviation industries there was a higher proportion of air reserve officers and similarly specialized reserve officers than there was in any other industry.

By 1927, the National Advisory Committee for Aeronautics had established itself in a position of worldwide pre-eminence in aeronautical research. Its reports had wide distribution. Organized primarily to conduct basic research separate from military research, much of the committee's activity still pertained to products that had military application.

As originally established by the Sixty-Third Congress in March, 1915, the facilities of the NACA were to provide service to any department or agency of the government that had an interest in aeronautics. But it was wisely permitted to exercise its functions for any individual, firm or association, provided the actual cost of the research was defrayed.

With this broad charter, the interrelation of industry, military, and civilian interests was enhanced in many ways. The research facilities and activities of universities and individual companies cannot be discounted, but they were always limited by how much funding was available. By having a national institution with ever increasing capability, competitive duplication was avoided and tremendous savings in time and effort were realized. In the same way that the cross-licensing arrangements of the Manufacturers Aircraft Association stimulated competition in a broader sense, the NACA research stimulated more rapid technical progress for all.

RESEARCH AND PRODUCTION

While it might be assumed that technical research, if progressive enough, could keep a nation abreast of competition without production of usable articles, several factors invalidate this assumption. Aircraft are such complex assemblies of technical components and materials that it is impossible to predetermine how the elements will work in untried combinations. Further, the manufacturing processes and techniques determine whether the forms and structural performances can be achieved in practice. Much of the ability to build an aircraft to certain standards depends upon the availability of specific tools, trained personnel, and assembly facilities. This is a long-term evolutionary process.

Innovation and experimentation is naturally a by-product of production. High rates of production require large technical staffs with the attendant inevitable generation of many ideas for improvement. These rates also involve extensive flight experience by test pilots and operators that reveals deficiencies and potential means for improving performance. When production is low, as it was in the 1930s, it is more critical that independent research maintain a flow of progress beyond what the manufacturers or operators can sustain. The NACA did this, and the ability to create a competitive force in an emergency was due in a major way to the activities of the committee. It was, in fact, a silent partner in all aviation activities.

With the popular preoccupation with specific types and models of aircraft, engines, and components, it is easy to miss the impact of the basic research function. Even when recognized, it usually appears to be simply the function of specific laboratories or personnel. One reason for the success of the NACA lies in its name, which really denotes an inspired concept. It *was* an "Advisory Committee." It had laboratories and technicians who were outstanding, but its committee function was significant in itself.

As its charter provided, the committee was composed of representatives of "departments and agencies of the Government," such as the Smithsonian, the

Bureau of Standards, and the Weather Bureau. It included representatives of the Army and Navy and of technical educational institutions and industry, as well as of airline or other civil operations activities. The members were always a distinguished and experienced group, who held positions of responsibility in their own fields. The committee reviewed programs and achievements and provided coordinated guidance for future policy.

Throughout the period prior to World War II, the director of Aero Research was George W. Lewis. He enjoyed the trust and respect of the military and the industry and apparently was also persuasive with Congress. John F. Victory was the secretary during this period. The initial laboratory was the Langley Laboratory at Langley Field, Virgina. Here, Henry J. E. Reid was the engineer in charge. Assuming this responsibility in the mid-1920s when a wind tunnel was *the* research tool, he was principally responsible for the rapid and impressive buildup of new test facilities.

RESEARCH FACILITIES

Most significant were the design and construction of the "variable density wind tunnel." Small models in slow moving airstreams had suffered from serious scale effects. A factor known as Reynolds Number related the dimension of the model and the viscosity of the air. If the air is visualized as being composed of definite particles, like ping-pong balls, it is obvious that there are few particles involved as the air moves at slow speed over a small model. In full scale at flight speeds, the aircraft impacts more of these particles because of both the dimensions of the aircraft and the speed with which it moves through the air. If the air is compressed in the tunnel, these imaginary particles are crowded closer together and, in moving past even a small model, tend to react more like the free air during the passage of a full-scale airplane.

Viscosity can be likened to the scrubbing action of these particles as they pass over the surface. The increase in density also effects this factor. With the "variable density tunnel," model test data became more reliable and realistic. Previously, empirical correction factors had to be obtained by comparing tunnel data with full-flight data for the same object. With variable density, good correlation between experimental data and flight began to be available quite early and in advance of most research worldwide.

A full-scale tunnel that could accept complete airplanes up to the size of fighters added another dimension. The real airplanes included details of construction and form that were difficult to reproduce in small scale. More important, it became possible to investigate modifications more quickly and at less risk than in free flight.

In the mid-1930s, a "spin tunnel" was developed. It provided a vertical rising column of air into which dynamic models could be introduced in spinning modes. Movable controls on the models could be actuated electronically from outside the tunnel to investigate recovery techniques.

An example of the value of this facility was graphically demonstrated by experience with the PB-2A. This low-wing monoplane had passed all acceptance tests and evaluations and was considered to be a very good flying and handling machine. However, a service ferry pilot picking up one of the first planes at the factory in 1935 inadvertenly entered a spin from which he was unable to recover. He and his passenger parachuted to safety, but a full-fledged investigation was begun at Wright Field. Although the aircraft was spun by a number of test pilots using a variety of techniques, it was impossible to duplicate the uncontrollable spin.

However, Harold M. ("Hez") McClelland, chief of the flight test section, continued the investigation. A spin model test in the new NACA facility eventually revealed that if a spin were entered with less control displacement than would have been normal for an intentional maneuver, recovery could not be achieved by normal recovery control techniques. Recovery required first that controls be actuated to produce a normal intentional spin and then that the rudder be applied for directional control. The result was the establishment of new standards for tail-surface configuration and new standard operating procedures for recoveries.

As additional research centers were established, the capacity and capability for research increased. Attempting to itemize all the contributions of the NACA would be futile. Any randomly selected area involving applied technology for airplanes, engines, or operations would inevitably reveal some dependence on a facet of NACA activity. Typical might be the development of low-drag cowling for radial, air-cooled engines that benefited aircraft and engines of many types and in many applications.

What was unique in the NACA was the scope and variety of the full-scale flight research. Although the military services, most companies, and the airlines maintained flight test activities, some of them quite extensive, the scope was somewhat limited. By nature, each service was primarily concerned with its own aircraft types, as were the companies and the airlines. Operational testing was conducted in accelerated service tests or in the development of advanced operating techniques. But the NACA operated planes from the Army and the Navy, as well as many civilian types. Beyond this, there were more basic investigations such as pressure distribution, handling, and stability that were intended to provide fundamental design parameters.

EXCHANGE OF TECHNICAL INFORMATION

What was more significant than the scores of reports and memoranda that presented conclusions and engineering data was the maintenance of an unusually competent and highly qualified staff of engineers and pilots. The element of experience and continuity has far reaching effects not always given adequate recognition. Working steadily over many years with hundreds of aircraft types and thousands of tests, the pilots and the engineers built up such a wealth of skill and experience that it is impossible to trace all the ways in which it was applied. In the simplest form, any pilot who has flown two or three hundred different aircraft, including specially built articles and peculiar modifications, has acquired a relative judgment that transcends the evaluation of a particular test. This gets applied to many situations, saves time and cost, and benefits the whole aviation fraternity. It was a major factor in spreading progress with a limited procurement and operational base.

Another opportunity for exchange of technical information occurred in the yearly meetings at the NACA laboratories. Here, representatives of the military services and industry were shown the facilities and briefed on programs in progress. Like all meetings of professional groups, the informal meetings between members in similar lines of work overleaped organizational limits and furthered the cross-fertilization of technical progress.

An intangible but real contribution was made by John Jay Ide, the technical assistant, Europe. His office provided a steady flow of information on foreign types and technical progress. While in no way representing a form of espionage, it did provide a channel for collecting and directing information that would have been available to United States manufacturers had they been able to maintain representatives abroad. Probably more data could be obtained by someone with official status than by private individuals. Export, particularly of transport types, also supplemented this exchange.

A listing of aircraft manufacturers tends to omit the builders of racing planes, who could have been individuals or small operations with five to ten helpers. Yet the E. M. ("Matty") Lairds, James R. ("Jimmy") Wedells, and B. O. ("Benny") Howards applied the latest aerodynamic principles to their one or two machines with startling results. The high performance of their products tended to pace the industry. It would be hard to evaluate the stimulus they provided or the training and experience that was involved. No less significant was their impact on engines, since all the racing engines were "souped up" versions modified by either individuals or the manufacturing companies.

There are many other cases where the contributions of unexpected sources to the creation of air power would not have been included in a statistical compilation of industrial and military size and activity. There were companies that, as a part of their product line, made items for aircraft; Winchester Arms made radiator tubes and radiators; A. O. Smith made steel propeller blades; wire rope manufacturers made aircraft cable; hydraulic fitting manufacturers made aircraft standard fittings; tire companies made aircraft tires; wheels and brakes came from a variety of sources that were not entirely aircraft suppliers.

The participation of this second and third layer was not apparent until expanded production was called for, but it existed and always will. How can the proportional effort in the manufacture of a critical aircraft forging be evaluated? The airplane company normally maintains a machine shop and machinists to do the final machining. The forging may come from the aluminum manufacturer. But the dies to make the forging may come from a specialized machine shop. And, of course, only a small portion of the output of a processor of a raw material such as aluminum, for instance, goes into aircraft production.

FUNDING

The same considerations apply to funding levels, inventories, military personnel strength, and dollar values. But disregarding the anomalies, there is little doubt that the military air establishment was small compared to what might have been expected as part of a reasonable defense posture. This was recognized early in the 1920s and reiterated frequently by boards and responsible politicians, but only in about 1936–37 was any effort made to correct the situation.

Some excerpts from the October, 1923, report of the Lassiter Committee appointed to investigate and report on the present status and future condition of the Air Service are interesting. For the regular Army, "There are now authorized 12,000 officers and 125,000 enlisted men of which the Air Service allotment is 1,061 officers and 8,764 enlisted men (including 190 flying cadets). Of these only 880 officers and 8,399 enlisted men and 91 flying cadets are now available (February 28, 1923)."

Further, "the peace organization of the Air Service now bears no relation to the war requirements and affords little or no foundation upon which war requirements in either personnel or materiel can be built." Amplifying the materiel situation, "The equipment situation is so critical that, with a continuance of appropriations at the present rate, by July 1926, there will be available less than 300 serviceable airplanes to meet a requirement of over five times that number . . ." "Furthermore, 80% of these airplanes are of an obsolescent training type or are unsuitable for combat use."

These conclusions would not be unexpected from a committee concerned with military preparedness. But it is necessary to understand the attitude of the country to realize that the situation should have been expected. Immediately after the "war to end all wars," there was a great rush to shut out all consideration of matters recalling the abhorrent last few years. Furthermore, there was a letdown economically connected with the readjustment to a peacetime economy. Business seemed to be looking up, but military appropriations would have been considered detractions from social and business programs.

For the next ten to twelve years, almost any annual report included statements almost paraphrasing the Lassiter report. Military personnel figures remained nearly constant, though the specific numbers for each year must be analyzed to see whether they included reserves on active duty, reserves on inactive status, cadets in training, National Guard for the Army and Marines for the Navy, pilot and nonpilot ratings, and civilian employees in maintenance, supply, and support positions.

Money values are equally uncertain unless each figure is scrutinized carefully for the breakdown into categories. For instance, the number of aircraft produced is probably accurate. With the wide variations in lead times, appropriations do not relate directly to orders, and orders do not relate directly to production or delivery. One order may take three to five years to complete while another may be completed in the same fiscal year. While commercial sales may be assumed to include engines and equipment unless noted otherwise, military aircraft sales probably exclude engines, some instruments, and much equipment purchased separately and supplied as government-furnished equipment (GFE). Military appropriations may include special one-time items for facilities, and they may include pay for military and civilian personnel. Presumably, appropriations for airmail primarily represent operating costs. Some portion will support the maintenance of technical operating staff, and some will go for procurement of aircraft, engines, or spares. However, much will be immediately channeled out into economic areas not directly connected with the aviation industry or aerial operations.

Sample tabulations are revealing and provide the basis for some interpretation. They show relative distributions of support or effort, as well as trends from which general conclusions can be drawn. Industry figures demonstrate that commercial aircraft were produced in larger numbers, but with much smaller dollar values, than military types were. Since commercial transport planes during the period being considered were high in cost and comparable to military planes, it must be assumed that a predominant portion of commercial production was light, small aircraft. Thus, although the numbers may be impressive, they do not support a major industry.

On the other hand, dollar figures for military aircraft may be misleading if a trend is plotted year by year. Discounting any inflationary trends, the dollar cost per military aircraft increased because of increasing demands for performance, increasing size and weight, and the continued practice of buying only small quantities. If pounds of aircraft procured were taken as the baseline and cost per pound were to be considered constant, then from the late 1920s to 1939 or 1940, the dollars should have increased threefold for any category such as bombers, observation aircraft, or fighters. Anything less would have meant a loss of combat readiness. This, of course, was the observed result.

Nevertheless, the total dollar value going into the industry from either civil or military purchases did support facilities, engineering, and manufacturing staff. Consequently, the *potential* capability did not suffer as much as might have been expected. Evidently, intangible factors are assessed more accurately by qualitative observation of those individuals involved at the time than by any amount of research or analysis of statistical data.

A CHANGE IN THE 1930s

A change took place about 1934, when government officials realized that procurement policy, political policy, and appropriations had not maintained either an industry or a force adequate for defense. Plans for considerable augmentation were created, but even after deliveries some two years hence, it was estimated that the United States would still be in fifth place among military powers.

The 1936 *Aircraft Year Book* described the situation at the beginning of 1935; "Several plants which the government would need badly in the event of an emergency, with its positive demands for thousands of combat planes as quickly as possible, have devoted their production to casual orders for military equipment in the past, and now have little, and in some cases, no business. Others are carrying on development work for the services at a loss. A few have profitable orders; and one or two companies are expanding."

By early 1936, the Air Corps had about 1,300 pilots, and the Navy about 1,200. The large reserve contingent of the Air Corps cannot be entirely discounted, but many of the active pilots were in civilian flying jobs, others were limited by a shortage of planes, and many officers were nonflying. The National Guard was better organized in units, but shortages of planes and funds limited their efficiency.

The Army had about 1,100 planes, and the Navy about 800. But it was estimated that of the 1,100 Army planes only about 300 were first-line combat types. Presumably, the Navy proportion of first-line types would have been similar. The estimates at the time were that about 4,000 planes were needed to provide a minimum force and that, although funds had begun to become available, it would take about four years for the industry and the forces to reach this sort of strength. In reality, the push to reach this kind of strength did not take place until about 1939.

Although a turning point was reached in 1936, the period of late 1933 saw a widespread interest in the status and future of aviation. Several committees of Congress initiated investigations. Numerous executive agencies conducted investigations, and the Baker Board, headed by Newton D. Baker, was formed in April, 1934, to evaluate the state of civil aviation, the manufacturing industry, and the military.

The conclusions of the Baker Board confirmed the obvious superiority of the civil airlines both in operations and in equipment compared with the rest of the world. In particular, it stressed that the manufacturing industry was inadequate to support the demands that would be put upon it to expand to meet a war emergency. It also set goals for enlarging the military air services. These findings were the same that every investigation over the last ten years had reached. There was no immediate reaction increasing support for the military, but such a report by a prestigious group probably helped to initiate the changes which took place some two to three years later. At the time, there was considerable preoccupation with the question of establishing a separate Air Force, which was rejected by the board.

The stream of investigators was an onerous distraction to the key people in the small and struggling industry. Whether any significant results came about from most of the investigations is doubtful. However, the Black Committee report in late 1933 became the basis for the cancellation of the airmail contracts in February, 1934. This action had a profound effect that is difficult to evaluate objectively. Certainly the press coverage and most of the conclusions at the time were erroneous. They were colored by the political implications and by a lack of accurate information. A few informed, and objective, reports and conclusions were toned down in a general desire to forget the whole episode.

Coincidence in history is always significant as it frequently reveals undocumented influences. In 1934, the airmail cancellations occurred in February; the Baker Board came into being in April; the airmail contracts were reinstated on a temporary basis in June. The state of military equipment and the results of two to three years of inadequate support for military operations and procurement had surfaced. The implications of improprieties in airline growth, subsidization, and route allocations began to backfire, almost as soon as the Air Corps started the operation.

It may well be that the drama accompanying the incident gave the recommendations of the Baker Board a credibility and acceptance not accorded any previous estimate of the situation since at least 1923. It certainly attracted political and public recognition of factors that previously had not been appreciated. There are grounds for assuming that this was a low point, and the revelation of all the deficiencies in the Air Corps and the state of the industry, as well as of the outstanding good points of the airline industry, started movement in a positive direction. What certainly seemed, at the time, to be a punitive action can be considered to have been a significant factor in putting the country in a position to meet the demands of war years.

If this short period of about three and one-half months is significant in the history of the whole aircraft establishment, it deserves more elaboration and appraisal than it has received. It is probably not possible to describe or define the event in detail, since it was reported so inaccurately at the time. Certainly, some of the summaries for popular consumption did little more than repeat the inaccuracies and the biased releases with unjustified conclusions.

However, some pertinent observations appear from the facts and are worth summarizing since they seem to be part of the preamble to the World War II expansion.

The airlines had built up a highly organized and effective system over a six to eight year period. They had purchased advanced equipment and were operating Boeing 247 transports; the first DC-2s were being delivered while the Air Corps was flying the mail. The industry had manufactured excellent aircraft for the purpose, and the prospects of more efficient and less costly service were in evidence. The last flights before cancellation indicated almost record-breaking performance and after reinstallation of commercial service, the performance boomed. The government's support of the airmail contracts had been a major factor in the buildup and was recognized as a legitimate form of subsidy.

Technical progress in the manufacturing industry would have fallen far behind had it not been for the stimulation of civil aviation, particularly the airline business. Even with the help of the airmail funding, the business was not really profitable, and reorganization and refinancing kept the struggling airlines going for a long time.

The airlines operated with highly qualified personnel. Some of the airlines hired only ex-military pilots or military-trained pilots. Continued training and the accumulation of extensive experience in the specialized operation over familiar routes built up a very high level of proficiency. Although there were probably instances of political influence in some of the past allocations of routes, the airline industry as a whole was neither rich enough nor powerful enough to exert any significant influence. Its inability to prevent the airmail contract's cancellation tends to substantiate this conclusion.

The Air Corps demonstrated an ability to deploy a major force to widely dispersed locations in just a few days. It had to establish temporary headquarters at each dispersed base. In view of the small number of permanent military bases in existence at the time and of the supply depot structure, the logistic support for the dispersed force was a major achievement. In the first deployment of aircraft to dispersed locations, there were mistakes in the allocation of aircraft types. For instance, two-place attack airplanes, A-12s, were originally sent to San Francisco. As the schedules were set, it became apparent that most of the flights were night flights over the mountains in winter weather. The airplanes were single-engined, designed for low-level, formation ground attacks during daylight, and were without 101 full night-flying provisions. They had to be reassigned and were replaced by twin-engined light bombers, such as the B-7, which were more suitable for the particular schedules.

The administrative and support functions were heavy burdens since all the personnel were on temporary duty and working with small temporary crews in makeshift quarters. Movement of personnel, supplies, and aircraft involved a lot of flying that supported the operation but did not directly move the mail. For instance, some bombers had to be retained at the supply depots to carry provisions such as replacement engines to grounded aircraft at the intermediate stations. Similarly, since transports such as tri-motor Fords and Fokkers were so few that they were assigned to other activities, they would have had little impact and were not available.

One of the facets receiving widespread publicity was the large number of accidents and the fatalities (twelve) that occurred during the 90-day period. The accounts lumped all mishaps into the same group. But most accidents did not involve carrying mail; many were due to extensive ferrying and random administrative flights. As a result, the phrase "and training" was added to most accounts. The executive order to the military to take over a nationwide civilian function had to be accepted by the military on the basis of urgency appropriate to any military emergency, even though it had probably not been intended to create a national emergency. The result was that many supporting activities were approached with the assumption of relatively high risk.

One particularly disturbing instance involved the fatal accident of J. B. Patrick, the base operations officer, at Barksdale Field. On a familiarization flight with the first P-26 assigned to the base, he had a forced landing in a rough field in east Texas. The all-metal low-wing monoplane nosed over, and Patrick was killed when the fuselage was crushed. This accident led to the requirement that all low-wing monoplanes have turn-over protection, but it had no direct relation to the airmail operation. The tragedy was used by the press to further a contention of Air Corps incompetence in airmail operations—to the resentment of military personnel.

Another factor that received a great deal of attention but now seems irrelevant was the cost of the Air Corps operation. Cost is usually disregarded in planning any action involving the use of military force in an emergency. It must have been recognized that using aircraft that were not well suited for the purpose, and personnel on detached or remote duty who were making do with temporary facilities and improvised logistics, would be much more expensive than the well-organized civilian operation that already had personnel and facilities in place.

Most of the Air Corps planes were biplanes with fabric-covered wings, some were entirely fabric-covered. They were obviously antiquated when compared with the airlines' single-engine Northrop and Lockheed planes, the Boeing 247, and the first DCs by Douglas. Even their Ford tri-motors appeared more modern than the strut-braced, all-metal A-12 attack aircraft and the light bomber B-7s of the Air Corps. Unlike the maneuvers of 1931, this comparison apparently impressed both the public and the politicians.

The Air Corps pilots had an opportunity to accumulate enough flying time to raise their proficiency. The active pilots probably flew more in the three months period than they had flown in the two years preceding. Many of the Air Corps pilots had friends who were flying for the airlines; some of these airline pilots had once served on active duty with the military units now flying the mail.

The winter weather at the start respected neither the airplanes' insignia nor the pilots' uniforms. Both civilian and military pilots sat out the bad spells, and both drove through the barely flyable. Even accidents were not confined to one service. For instance, at Salt Lake City in a spell of bad weather late in February, while most flights were grounded and the Air Corps was awaiting improvement in the weather, a passenger transport took off, hoping to get through to Cheyenne. The gesture seemed futile, and a few moments later, the plane crashed amid snow and ice against the mountains a few miles to the east. All the civilian passengers and the airline crew perished.

The operation of the instrument-landing transition training at Wright Field summarizes the situation. The first production Martin B-10 bombers were picked up at the factory and flown to Wright Field for the installation of electronic gear for blind landing. Eighteen pilots were assigned for training in March. After starting on BT-2 training planes previously used in instrument flight and landing development, the pilots were transferred to the B-10s. In just under 60 days, some 760 hooded blind landings were made. The final flight check involved a cross-country flight from Dayton to Indianapolis and Chicago and back, with the whole flight on instruments including takeoff and landing. Not only were the planes equipped and the pilots trained, but the ground guiding stations were built and being deployed across the country when the airmail was turned back to the airlines at the end of May.

In addition to the pilots in training were the instructors under the direction of Albert F. Hegenberger, giving a total of about 25 pilots who were as skilled in instrument flying as any pilots in the world. Only slightly behind were the pilots from the navigation school at Rockwell Field in San Diego who had been making extended over-water flights, relying completely on instruments. The flying schools had instructor pilots, well qualified in instrument flying. These pilots were assigned to the mail routes. Overall, fewer than fifty pilots had this degree of proficiency. The B-10s were all-metal monoplanes with performance equal to those of the advanced airline transports.

The capability was there to respond in an incredibly short time. The quality of performance was outstanding for the time. But the quantity was dangerously restricted. The same characterization could have been applied to the Air Corps's organization and operation as a whole. It reflected the overall status of the corps and, indeed, of the whole military stature of the period.

An interesting sidelight was provided by a visit in early May of Clarence Chamberlin, a member of the Baker Board, to the blind-landing operation at Wright Field. Even though he observed the cross-country flights in B-10s and the hooded landings, he expressed skepticism. However, he was aware of the work and the progress, and his observations may have influenced the board findings. Doolittle was also on the board, and from his pioneering with the Guggenheim Fog Flying Laboratory, he was in a position to appreciate the accomplishment.

NEW PROCUREMENT POLICIES

The procurement procedures were then modified by congressional directive, and very substantial increases in appropriations were forthcoming.

The airlines were forced to reorganize and get rid of officials who had been key figures in the earlier allocations of routes and rates. Whether this was a face-saving gesture or had real significance is a moot question. It is reasonable to assume that, in spite of temporary hardship, the transport industry was stronger and more secure afterward. The period of early mergers in 1930 was completed at this time, creating very nearly the composition that has since existed. A number of short haul routes were initiated at the same time.

Certainly, the manufacturing industry, after suffering some setback from the airline loss of income, had an increasing and more substantial market in transport aircraft.

With the recognized need to modernize the military services, and with the more adequate funding that soon followed, the relationship between the military and the manufacturing industry grew stronger.

There was no evidence that the original Black Committee findings or the cancellation of the mail contracts were deviously planned to benefit the military air services, the industry, or the airlines. That this happened must be considered to be more than chance, however. There has always seemed to be an opportunist characteristic of those connected with aviation to outmaneuver mishap and to turn adversity to advantage.

In Congress, there were some men who supported a realistically adequate defense and saw the importance of air power. These individuals, such as Representative Carl Vinson and Representative J. J. McSwain, were now able to provide the necessary help and guidance. The airlines were largely absolved of wrongdoing, and the value of their activity was finally recognized. The Air Corps had demonstrated a capability to perform its assigned mission of mobilizing, deploying forces on short notice, and performing creditably with what equipment and personnel it had. The relative modernity of the later transport types and their excellent performance indicated the ability of the manufacturing industry to produce high-quality products even in small numbers. Of course, all the performance potential had to reflect a high degree of technical competence backed by a substantial reservoir of research.

The whole aviation activity involves considerable lead time. Research depends on design and manufacture to appear in flying form. Manufacture depends first on funding to initiate contracts and then on construction time to produce planes. Funding depends on profits or advance financing in commercal operations and on requirements and appropriations in the military. So if 1934 was a low point, it might be expected that the downward momentum would take time to reverse. In the meantime, the manufacturers could die of starvation. Nevertheless, the appropriation figures up to 1940 indicate some trends from which inferences can be drawn. Short-term changes from year to year or from category to category require detailed analysis to reach accurate conclusions, but the trends do confirm generally observed conditions.

These figures cannot be used as precise data because many of them require explanatory footnotes. Supplementary appropriations may be included, and unexpended funds may have been returned. There are many explanations of extraordinary expenditures. The figures as shown here do, however, provide qualitative values for determining trends and relative distribution.

The steady buildup in money given the Army from 1911 to 1916 reflects a gradual increase in the appreciation of the function of aerial observation as a supplement to ground action. In the early years, there was little application for air in a predominately surface Navy. With the onset of World War I, the Navy found long-range patrol and lighter-than-air aircraft a valuable adjunct.

After the cancellations and cutbacks at the conclusion of the war, the Army coasted on surplus aircraft with a diminishing personnel roster. The Navy, however, was just finding the utility of aircraft with the fleet. The growing requirement for aircraft to equip carriers and the growing concept of carrier task-force operations stimulated a stronger support than that for the Air Corps right through the period, until about 1936.

The growing subsidization of the airline industry through airmail appropriations shows clearly up to 1931–32, when the airmail appropriation almost equaled that for the Navy or the Army. This reflected the rapid increase in the usefulness of commercial air transport more than any planned effort to stimulate a particular industry artificially. It did serve to follow the growth with support that benefited both the operators and the manufacturers.

The appropriation for the Commerce Department indicated a very rapid increase in support for airways and in regulations supporting civil aviation. There were benefits from this increased activity in that it maintained a portion of the manufacturing industry. Any development of aviation in general had secondary and collateral effects on the mobilization potential. For instance, civilian flying schools were able to expand to create a major base for the training of pilots in preparation for the war expansion.

An interesting point is the figure for 1923–24 for the Air Corps. This low point suggests the reason for the concern of the Lassiter Board and its strong language describing the impotence of the Air Corps as a defense force.

The economic crash and Depression of 1929 had an immediate effect on business and commerce, but there was an "aftershock" of broader and deeper impact

AIRCRAFT APPROPRIATIONS 1898 to 1940

	Army	Navy	Air Mail	NACA	Commerce
1898	$ 25,000 (Langley)				
1899	25,000 (Langley)				
1908	25,000 (Wright)				
1909	5,000 (Wright)				
1911–12	125,000	$ 25,000			
1913	100,000	10,000			
1914	175,000	10,000			
1915	200,000	10,000		$ 5,000	
1916	800,000	1,000,000		5,000	
1917	18,081,666	3,500,000	$ 1,060,000	87,516	
1918	50,410,000	61,133,000	100,000	112,000	
1919	467,304,758	123,383,119	100,000	205,000	
1920	25,000,000	25,000,000	850,000	175,000	
1921	33,000,000	20,000,000	1,250,000	210,000	
1921–22	19,200,000	13,413,431	1,250,000	200,000	
1922–23	12,895,000	14,683,590	1,900,000	210,000	
1923–24	12,426,000	14,647,174	1,500,000	283,000	
1924–25	13,476,619	15,150,000		470,000	
1925–26	18,061,191	15,130,000	500,000	534,000	
1926–27	18,256,694	19,065,288	2,000,000	513,000	$ 550,000
1927–28	25,612,494	20,100,000	4,650,000	550,000	3,791,500
1928–29	33,911,431	32,189,000	14,480,000	628,770	5,519,350
1929–30	34,910,059	31,430,000	19,300,000	1,508,000	6,416,620
1930–31	38,892,968	32,033,211	24,600,000	1,321,000	9,204,830
1931–32	31,850,892	31,145,000	27,000,000	1,051,070	10,362,300
1932–33	25,673,236	32,745,420	26,460,000	920,000	8,553,500
1933–34	34,037,769	21,957,459	22,000,000	695,000	7,660,780
1934–35	30,917,702	34,842,253	19,003,291	726,492	5,681,029
1935–36	50,287,197	40,732,310	18,700,000	1,177,550	5,909,800
1936–37	62,607,727	38,588,270	20,230,000	2,544,550	6,850,000
1937–38	67,308,374	49,500,000	24,405,860	1,733,850	13,238,500
1938–39	73,799,532	48,074,000	27,592,275	2,508,000	16,231,130(CAA)
1939–40	320,447,529	111,459,000	31,162,720	6,543,080	25,768,000(CAA)

occurring about 1932. The result was felt unevenly throughout the economy, and the same unevenness was apparent in the appropriation summaries.

The impact on the airlines of the cancellations of mail contracts in 1934 shows clearly in these figures though it was attenuated somewhat by reduced appropriations in later years. Perhaps the increasing ability of the airlines to exist with less government support also explains a lesser rate of growth in appropriations, even though the actual operations grew tremendously.

The 1933–34 figure for the Air Corps may reflect the costs of the airmail and the transfer of funds to cover the extraordinary expenses. However, if costs are averaged out, it is clear that the beginning of recognition of the need for a military air force occurred in 1936 and continued to 1939, when the war in Europe justified the big across-the-board increase in 1939–40.

In covering the interrelationship between the various elements that made up the total *base* for air power in the 1930s, little reference has been made to the changing organization of the air arms of the Army and Navy. There are two reasons for this. One is that as the internal relationships changed within the services, the impacts were felt primarily in political and high-level military quarters. At the lower working levels, although there was always concern over the status of the service, technical and operational problems and progress did not seem to change with organizational shifts. The other factor was that relations between the military services and the civilian sector were primarily dependent on appropriations and overall political support rather than on the form of the hierarchy. In the total framework of air power, it is, of course, important to consider in depth the significance of the command structure. But this is a large subject in itself and deserves elaboration within its own frame of reference.

SEEDS OF GROWTH

For the accelerated expansion that began in 1940 to have taken place, the seeds for its growth must have been planted by 1935 or 1936. Certainly, no one in the establishment at the time would have guessed that the struggle for bare existence of U.S. air power was more than just barely holding the line. To many, the prospects for recognition and support seemed hopeless. The superficial aspects of the airmail episode were depressing. Even the revisions in procurement procedures created difficulties, although, in retrospect, they probably provided the element of confidence upon which increasing appropriations were based.

Each company and organization has a history, and those whose stories have been published tried to show that their contribution was critical and provided the basis for future success in the face of difficulties and competition. Of course, everyone involved in the growth of air power suffered from similar problems and could only have advanced by some indefinite cooperation. It would be unreasonable to accord credit to any one circumstance. Only a most fortunate coincidence of many factors could have carried the whole activity through the mid-1930s and have started a new effort in a form capable of meeting the stresses of expansion.

By either monetary or personnel standards, the whole aviation community, both military and civilian, was small. It is only necessary to take the 1934 or 1935 production and delivery figures to realize how small a plant and how few people could be supported. If 10 percent of the officer strength of the Air Corps and Navy Air is taken as the force engaged in technical procurement and top-level directive activities, it becomes evident that this, too, was a very small group. It was certainly true that as expansion took place from 1938 on, it became increasingly difficult to get things done quickly.

Two factors, more than any others, coincided at the critical time. In spite of the meager introduction of transient aircraft forms in the early 1930s, rapid obsolescence of existing inventories created a demand for advanced and higher performance replacement. As a result, the military could set higher goals requiring new designs of much higher performance potential. With the assurance of some increasing business, the industry was able to cooperate with the military in creating prototypes of truly advanced designs in the later period.

A new generation of dedicated and enthusiastic engineers and pilots began to appear by the mid-1930s to reinforce the efforts of the pioneers who had carried the burden of frustration and discouragement through the late 1920s and early 1930s. A very close relationship existed between the civilian sector and the military. In spite of this, or perhaps because of it, patriotism and integrity were accepted as universal guiding principles, and any charge of improperly using this relationship would have been automatically challenged. In the final analysis, the people who maintained the capability to meet the crisis also implemented the reaction to the demands.

The most significant observation evident from the review of the status of the military and the industry is that the worst prognostications of boards were clearly demonstrated. It took two years to turn the downswing around. It also took two years to expand to a barely effective level and an additional two years to reach a strength that offered the possibility of survival and victory. Dedication and perseverance of "establishment" were not enough. There just was not enough support for military air power from 1922 to 1938 to sustain the nation in a minimum state of preparedness.

VI THE TASK OF PROCUREMENT

Perhaps the most important conclusion to be drawn from the history of twenty years of aircraft procurement is that no conclusions can be drawn; there are no formulas, no cut and dried rules to follow in every case. Procurement methods that work in one era may be utterly unworkable in another. The corporate character of the industry changes, the mood of the Congress changes, and a new President enters the White House . . . . The same congressmen who insisted upon stringent economy in 1934 may well have voted billions for defense while joining the clamor for negotiated contracts to speed the placement of contracts in 1941.

—Irving Briton Holley, Jr.
Buying Aircraft: Materiel Procurement for the Army Air Forces (1964)

Irving Holley accurately appraised the historical side of the problem of aircraft procurement in his masterfully compiled *Buying Aircraft*, but he failed to provide insight into the problems and processes by which those actually engaged in procurement managed to get planes and equipment. Almost every case was unique in some respect. The problem that had to be solved was how to get the quality and quantity within the limits imposed by law, by regulations, by the budget, and by the interpretation of the law by numerous federal agencies.

With each method of buying equipment—negotiation, sole source, price competition over a standard item, design competition, change order, and other variations— there were always enough objections that it was possible to find fault and contend that some other approach would have been preferable. So all development and procurement officers worked under the pressure of being wrong, at least as interpreted in some quarters.

QUALITY VERSUS PRICE

A "fantasy land" aspect exists in all competitive procurements with public funds where collusion and graft are potential threats. Conflict between quality and price is always present. Each reviewing agency and the legislative overseers view each instance from narrow and mutually exclusive points of view.

Assuming that competition is a goal that should be sought, the terms of the competition must be broad enough not only to permit the eminently qualified bidder to enter but also to entice the unexpected bidder and the novel solution. Although a well-defined solution is desired, a specification must be issued in such general terms that a bidder is dared to translate these terms back into a specific description of the desired article. Sometimes, the resulting proposal fails to represent the article that was the basis for the procuring agency's generalized statement.

When, in 1935, a multi-engine bomber competition was held, the four-engine design that Boeing submitted was certainly the kind of machine the military planners desired. But after the Boeing entry crashed before the completion of its required tests, the strict limitation of the competition prevented awarding a production contract to the company. Instead, the markedly inferior Douglas design won by default.

Also in 1935, when competition for transport planes was held, the bidders included Fairchild with the XC-31; Curtiss with a cargo-door version of the commercial Condor, a large twin-engine, single-bay biplane; and Douglas with a cargo modification of the DC-2 that was being used by the airlines. The Fairchild was a large single-engine, high-wing monoplane. It had a metal framework and was largely fabric covered. This plane followed the tradition that had been started with the Douglas C-1, a modification of the World Cruisers powered with a Liberty engine, and followed by a Bellanca and later a Fokker. The XC-31 had been built as an experimental procurement and was a good example of the traditional, evolutionary type. But it had a single engine and represented a form that was rapidly becoming obsolescent.

A larger derivative of the World Cruiser and 0-2, the C-1 was the first military transport ordered by the Army from Douglas.

Only one Kreider-Reisner XC-31 high-wing military cargo monoplane was ever built.

Like its civilian counterpart, the Curtiss military Condor was a two-engine plane, but like the Fairchild, it was also a disappearing type of aircraft, although it met the stated requirements.

The Douglas DC-2 was a more modern two-engine, all-metal monoplane representing emerging new configuration and construction concepts that offered superior performance. But the Douglas cost nearly twice as much as the other planes.

In this particular competition, the announced terms permitted the consideration of contenders other than the lowest bidder, so Douglas initially won the contract because it represented the sort of *quality* plane the operational evaluators wanted.

The secretary of war approved the quality selection, but the General Accounting Office contended that price should have been the deciding factor. In spite of the discretionary powers permitted the secretary by the 1926 law, payment was held up. It was almost two years before the conflict was settled and Douglas could be paid.

While the basic terms describing the articles desired are usually assumed to be contained in a document called a "type specification," there are literally hundreds of additional items in the accompanying "request for bids" defining specific materials, equipment, processes, and standard procedures for design and assumptions. Since not all unsatisfactory approaches or details can be specifically prohibited and not all new processes, features, and materials can be anticipated, some general phrases are stated or implied. For instance, though "good practice" and "state of the art" may seem to be too vague, there was little uncertainty about what the terms meant in communication between legitimate constructors and procurement agencies.

The most serious problems arose over "negotiated" procurement. It was recognized in the 1926 laws that there were aspects of procurement of technologically complex articles such as aircraft that could not be reduced to simple competitive bidding. In these cases, the source was selected by a variety of means, and then the performance and price were negotiated between the contractor and the procuring agency. This left room for complaint, argument, and charges of favoritism or collusion from political elements and disappointed suppliers. There were continual modifications in regulations and procedures that attempted to allay concerns and to provide a fair distribution of work while stimulating progress and insuring quality.

A SOLUTION

In 1934, the charges and restraints reached a peak. Most of the investigations into improprieties concluded that the interests of the government had been protected and that there was no real evidence of profiteering or of official malfeasance. Nevertheless, the original claims and charges always received publicity, while the sober conclusions were usually neglected or discounted. Two procedures were devised to take the heat off. These were the "design competition" and the "sample article" formula. In the first, preliminary but complete designs were submitted and evaluated and various forms of contracts were, or could be, awarded to the winner or winners. Presumably, if these were carried through to completion, an experimental article resulted, with the devlopment costs covered by the government. In the "sample article" form, the bidder had to submit a prototype, which was evaluated along with the technical data; the result was a contract for *quantity* procurement. The cost to each bidder was high, and losers stood little chance of recovering expenses. Both forms had significant disadvantages as well as benefits, but the forms themselves permitted some freedom.

The essential element in any of these forms was the establishment of formal evaluation procedures that had to satisfy all levels of review, including Congress. It would appear that at the time and in subsequent historical review, there was little appreciation of the philosophy that was the basis for the formal documentation. The most commonly made error occurred in interpretating the type specification that defined the performance. The performance figures and some of the other factors (for instance, armament) were expressed as "minimum acceptable," "desired," or somewhere within the considerable spread between these two extremes.

The "minimum" values had to represent an attainable aircraft but yet exclude a simple price bid on an article already in production. Therefore, these figures represented an advanced modification of something that was already in production or that a competitor could produce by using established designs, power plants, and equipment details. The minimum figures in the type specification could be considered to represent a balanced and complete aircraft.

On the other hand, the "desired" figures taken together did not in any sense represent an actual aircraft. In each category, such as high speed, the desired figure represented a difficult-to-reach level obtained from analysis of many design studies made in-house. Coupled with the evaluation procedure in which no points of merit were awarded for exceeding the desired figure, it helped designers to avoid distorting designs by maximizing one factor at the expense of utility in other characteristics. It would have been normal for the winner's specification to fall between the minimum and the desired values; in most cases, this actually happened. The term *desired* may appear to have been misleading, but it was explained to bidders; and the method of evaluation served to strengthen the implications. A common misconception was that a winner *failed* to meet the desired figures. Actually, this was the intent of the procedure; a designer could not reach the desired levels with any extension of the state of the art as it existed at the time.

The companion piece to the type specification in the bid data was a method of evaluation. There was always an expressed difference of opinion between the Navy and the Air Corps and among various factions in the procurement chain about the desirability or validity of any numerical appraisal. There was particular objection to the issuance of the weighting figures assigned to the various categories of design data. However, the process seemed to satisfy the political objections at the time, at least as far as Air Corps procurement was concerned. There were some other residual benefits that permitted getting quality even at somewhat higher prices.

But as in the case of the type specification, a casual examination of the evaluation fails to reveal the philosophy that made it work. By carefully coordinating the spread of minimum and desired figures and the points of merit available in each category, it was possible to imply where emphasis should be placed. It was obviously counterproductive for the procurement agency to keep the bidders in the dark about what characteristics were to be considered important.

There had to be some escape clauses. They were vitally important and answered many of the objections to the system, although they were largely overlooked by critics. One such clause stipulated that whenever any factor in a particular category (for instance, structures) was so questionable that it threw doubt on the credibility of the whole design, *all* the points in *that* category could be deducted. This favored conservative, carefully designed bids and discouraged outrageously optimistic proposals. At the same time, it relieved the evaluators of the nearly impossible job of justifying, in detail, relative superiority of one marginal design over another. More significantly, it confined the penalty to the category being considered so that there was a limit to the number of penalties that could be applied by one specialist on the evaluation team.

Another clause was actually contained in a "factor of substantiation" to which a carefully determined number of points was assigned. When bidders submitted guaranteed performance or weight figures and the reviewing technicians could not accept the assumptions that led to the figures, the evaluators recomputed comparative figures for all the contenders. Legally, these new figures could not be substituted for the bidder's *guaranteed* ones without destroying the validity of the competition. The bidders contended logically that their engineers were as good as anybody else and that only after the article had been built and delivered could the differences be reconciled. There was also the possibility that individual prejudices could influence the recomputations. But the revised figures made by the *one* expert team using *one* set of procedures and assumptions for all bids did give a relative standing. They translated any discrepancy into a question of substantiation of the bid data either by test data or by past performance of an aircraft, and the relative number of points assigned in this category did in fact differentiate between conservative and optimistic proposals.

The Wright Field project officers, being the usual recorders for the boards, tried occasionally to see if biased reassignment of merit figures could change the relative standings enough to throw out a winner or select one of the losers. It proved to be almost impossible to alter relative standings by downgrading the weak points in a winner's score or upgrading strong points in a loser's. This occurred because of the limitations in availability of points in any one category and because of the inevitable cumulative effect that resulted from relative excellence in all aspects of the truly good and balanced design. While no selection process ever completely eliminated the discussions over a good armament installation versus an unusual high speed, objectors could be dared to alter their appraisal enough to invalidate the selections.

Furthermore, the procedure had been in the hands of the designers and bidders, and it was normal for them to run their own evaluations to maximize their own bids; so they had a pretty good idea of what their own final standings might be. In any event, the complete rules of the competition and judging were established before hand.

Another potential benefit was obtained from this procedure. By having numerical standings against which to compare price, it was possible to get a dollars-per-point-of-merit figure—in other words, a price per unit of quality. This did not work in cases such as the transport competition where the price spread was so great and where all the contenders substantially met the requirements, albeit with a spread in the quality ratings. But in the competitions where all the contenders represented about the same state of the art and the same state of development, the price per point did justify selecting the superior article even if its cost was higher.

There was always a category of "tactical or operational suitability" determined by a board of operational evaluators selected for a specific competition. This category tended to be overriding, but it had to be reinforced by good standings in the purely technical areas. In general, it was almost axiomatic that the operational evaluators got their preferred selection.

PLANNING AHEAD

There was always one difficulty that existed throughout the period of scarcity of funds, right up to the 1939–40 expansion programs. Normal budgeting procedure required that funds be set up about two years in advance, based on estimates of need, performance, and then-existing construction costs. This was always distorted by political considerations that stemmed from the desire to overcome numbers deficiencies in the inventory. So estimates of the number of planes to be procured with allocated funds always exceeded the numbers of aircraft that could actually be purchased later when the competitions were held. The numbers of planes "to be obtained" were usually considered firm in political planning and in the higher Army circles. Frequently, differences had to be reconciled when winning articles fell short of the replacement goals. This is probably a universal, timeless situation accentuated in every time period by all sorts of inflationary influences.

To the uninitiated observer, it must always seem that one three-view drawing of a proposed airplane is as good as another. Even to the more knowledgeable person, there is a feeling that only the physical article, flown and operated in test and service environments, reveals the quality and suitability. To a certain extent, this is true. But valid conclusions can be drawn from logic and experience so that any proposal can achieve its potential with only the usual correction of bugs and relatively minor modifications. While this appraisal may seem intuitive, it is actually quite precise. It is not necessary to "fly before buy," to quote a cliché from a later time. Where the configurations, weight, balance, power, and controls follow conventional patterns, details need only be examined to ensure that the expected characteristics will not be degraded in the actual fabrication. Where the proposals are more exotic or advanced, it becomes necessary to fall back on more basic aerodynamic and structural considerations. But even in these cases, the conclusions can be quite accurate and precise. The same application of skilled judgment applies in cost estimates and in operational suitability matters. In each instance, everything depends on the experience, judgment, and skill of the service engineers and officers doing the appraisals.

This appraisal is applied to all designs being considered with the degree of application dependent on how unusual the design is and on its state of development. In the design competition for the two-engine interceptor that resulted in the Lockheed XP-38, the performance was unusually high for the time, and the configuration was also unusual; so this appraisal process was exemplified dramatically.

PROPOSAL AND PERFORMANCE

Some of the design compromises that led to the relative confidence that the Lockheed proposal could achieve its performance estimates warrant detailed explanation.

Requirements for high-speed capability typically dictate a small machine. For any gross weight, this means a *high* wing loading (gross weight divided by square feet of wing area). To attain the high speed, with a high wing loading, the installed power must be great. This corresponds to a *low* power loading (gross weight divided by horsepower). The use of two engines automatically produces an airplane that is about one and ones half times the size and weight of a corresponding single-engine version.

The proposed design for the Lockheed plane had a high wing loading, higher than all but overloaded record-breaking articles of the time. But its power loading was unusually low, which partially offset the normal unsatisfactory maneuvering characteristics expected of heavy small aircraft.

The use of turbosuperchargers allowed the power to be maintained up to a critical altitude of 20,000 feet. By delivering full power from ground level up to this altitude, the high speed would increase about 1 percent per thousand feet so that maximum-speed altitude would be high. But turning performance, climb, and ceiling all depended on aerodynamic qualities as well as power. High wing loadings would have tended to degrade these factors.

"Climb" and "turn" are the same thing, as far as the wing is concerned. In a turn, the wing is climbing around a circle against centrifugal force instead of straight ahead against gravity. Here, the wing is at high lift angles with high drag; so efficiency tends to fall off rapidly with high wing loadings despite a plane's power. 113

The essence of aerodynamic efficiency is to work a lot of air gently instead of a smaller amount at high intensity. In order for the wing to impact a large number of air particles, it must reach well out to the sides to touch them in passing. Or by going faster, it can touch a correspondingly high number of air particles within a given time simply by running into more while going straight ahead.

In turns or climb, a plane's drag tends to be high, and its speed tends to decrease; so the compensating solution is to increase the wingspan. For any one wing area, increasing the span decreases the width (chord), which gives a higher span-to-chord ratio called the "aspect ratio." Sometimes, engineers use a ratio of weight to span called "span loading," which obviously is low with high-aspect ratios and vice versa.

At high altitude, air density decreases dramatically. A plane's lift decreases, but so does its drag; so as long as power can be maintained, the increasing speed tends to compensate. Of course, the higher speed requires larger radii for turns, but the relative performance compared with other planes in combat stays constant. Above the engine's critical altitude, where the power begins decreasing, only improved aerodynamic design efficiency can help turn, climb, and ceiling.

A clear understanding of the effect of aspect ratio or span loading is necessary to appreciate what was perhaps the most significant and unconventional item in the P-38 configuration. The aspect ratio of the proposed P-38 was 8 where it would be expected to be 6 or less. Due to the high accelerations achieved by large values of excess lift in fighting maneuvers, fighter designers tended to cut down on span to avoid difficult structural design problems.

Incidentally, there is a familiar and down-to-earth comparison that can clarify the situation for those who are not aeronautical engineers. On soft ground, wheeled vehicles are concerned with something called "flotation." Wide tires spread the load over a wider area as they roll forward; so they sink in less. Narrow tires at the same speed sink in farther or conversely have to go faster in order not to sink in more than the wider tires do. The depth of sinking creates a wall ahead of the wheel that must be climbed over; this is the same power absorber as climb in an aircraft.

As the ground becomes softer, or more fluid, the speed has to be increased regardless of tire width to avoid bogging down or stalling. The additional speed requires additional power for the speed as well as the climb. At some speed, the vehicle with narrow tires runs out of power to overcome both the climb and speed requirements. The wider tire may go to a higher speed requiring more power before it too reaches its ceiling and bogs down.

The P-38 proposal with its higher-than-usual aspect ratio and its span loading that was not very different from conventional fighters promised to be competitive. It could gain the advantages of high wing loading for speed and still not lose in maneuver and ceiling.

Rolling into and out of turns with alacrity is an essential factor in maneuvering fighters. Therefore, rate of roll becomes a major consideration. A large wingspan tends to degrade a plane's rolling rate because the wing surface is so far out from the fuselage and center of gravity. Making the wing tips narrower by tapering the plan form helps. The P-38 had a taper ratio of 3, with its tip being only one-third as wide as its root. Normal configurations would have had a taper ratio of about 2. This tended to offset what might have been expected to be a serious rolling rate disadvantage of a large-span plane.

Power as a factor in itself is only part of the story. It must be converted into usable thrust. This is particularly difficult to do efficiently in a small, high-speed plane. A plane of this type may have a lot of power, but the diameter of its propeller is limited by the tip speed, which combines both rotational and forward speed. It would be nice if its propeller's size could be increased to absorb the power by simply increasing its span, or diameter, to take advantage of the same efficiency considerations that apply to a wing. But tip speeds become extremely inefficient at or above the speed of sound.

The power, then, must be absorbed by increasing either the width or number of the blades, and the result of working more intensely on the volume of air flowing through the propeller disc brings about the same sort of inherent inefficiency as the high wing-loading, low aspect-ratio wing. This requires compromising performance at either the low-speed or high-speed end of the performance range.

Because the P-38's available power was put in two packages, its two propellers could absorb their share of the power as efficiently as might be expected with lower-powered planes at slower speeds. The increased propeller disc area assured that the plane's power and thrust would hold up throughout the maneuvering range.

The benefits of thrust efficiency were also felt in the plane's acceleration and takeoff performance. Nevertheless, high wing loadings normally result in high takeoff and landing speeds, which can be disadvantageous in combat aircraft.

Wing flaps were, of course, normal design additions by 1936 and were included in planes to compensate for the high speeds of takeoff and landing. But Lockheed went further by proposing a Fowler flap. This type of flap moves back from the wing to increase the wing area for the first part of its motion before its droops down to increase the curvature for higher lift, but with increased drag. The half extension was to be used for takeoff, and the full extension for landing.

Any airplane on the ground is definitely out of its element. In particular, small and fast planes are apt to be tricky and to require skillful control and handling. The P-38's stable tricycle landing gear removed most of this objection, and its wide tread further helped make it docile and tractable for taxiing, takeoff, and landing.

The geometry of the form indicated a long tail length, the number of times the average chord (width) of the wing goes into the distance from the center of gravity back to the tail surfaces. For a close-coupled small plane, this was normally a figure of 2 to 2½. For the proposed plane, this length was about 4. The expected result was increased "damping," a tendency to slow the rate of departure from a trimmed position caused by either gusts or intentional maneuvering, which suggested a potentially steady gun platform.

The long tail length required a smaller-than-normal tail surface area because of the increased arm at which the surface worked. Like many of Fokker's designs, this arrangement reduced drag and yielded an excellent flying airplane. The width of its horizontal tail was determined by the spacing of the booms. These were set by the width of the center body and the propeller diameters. The result was a very high aspect ratio for the horizontal surface. The end-plate effect of the two vertical fin and rudder surfaces on the booms produced an aerodynamic *apparent* aspect ratio that was even higher.

One effect of high aspect-ratio tails is to provide more rapid changes in force with small changes in an aircraft's angle of attack. This greater sensitivity, combined with the improved damping due to tail length, meant that less trimming force was necessary for stability and that there was a wider range of center of gravity position or stability available without degradation of flying characteristics.

The high aspect ratio of the horizontal tail also produced narrow chord elevators, which in turn meant relatively light control forces for maneuver. The tail length promised somewhat the same considerations for the vertical surfaces and rudders.

An added feature was the use of opposite rotation engines. Their symetrical flow of the slip streams eliminated carrying rudder displacement, with its attendant drag, for directional trim. Further, there was no change in trim with changes in speed,

Designed as a high-altitude interceptor, the Lockheed P-38 adopted a twin-engine configuration to provide sufficient performance. As Fighter Project officer, Kelsey conducted its first flight and was instrumental in its testing.

which promised enhanced quality for the gun platform in maneuvering flight.

A heavy airplane with a long-span wing would naturally be difficult to accelerate in a roll. The taper ratio might help some. But because of the plane's weight, the relatively small wing would mean small ailerons, while achieving high rates of roll would require generating relatively large forces. This in turn would mean relatively large aileron displacements with correspondingly high control forces felt by the pilot. For the P-38, flight testing was necessary to determine whether this dilemma was satisfactorily resolved. In practice, pilots who were sufficiently demanding and forceful got adequate response, but the high control forces remained a deficiency until hydraulic boost, the equivalent of power steering, was added.

Such a qualitative evaluation could be, and was, applied in varying degrees to all proposals for new military aircraft, regardless of type. It was always possible to deduce a close approximation of the expected characteristics of an airplane without having a physical article to evaluate. However, only meticulous quantitative analysis can indicate how closely predicted weight and aerodynamic performance will be met. The service laboratory staffs always made their own estimates from detailed structural drawings and specific wind tunnel or other basic aerodynamic data. These data came from all similar applications representing the state of the art at the time and in a large measure were independent of the particular articles under consideration. The combination of these factors was the primary reason why progress and judicious selection could be maintained during the sparse years without a larger number of actual airplanes entering the inventory.

THE FINISHED PLANE

The final proof was in the finished plane. It had to demonstrate the degree to which it developed its potential in an actual flight test. Besides the usual "bugs" associated with the first assembly of a large number of sophisticated elements in one package, there were always unexpected features that resulted from operations in new regimes.

A military aircraft requires unusually good accessibility to interior installations for maintenance, repair, and adjustment of equipment installations. These can only be evaluated with service experience. The military armament is at least half of the total equipment, and a good vehicle lacking in military suitability is worthless. But the detailed drawings provide a good estimate of the potential suitability, if good practice is used in construction details.

The P-38 illustrated several of these practical factors. One reason for using this aircraft as an illustration is that there are a large number of excellent popular references describing its development and operation.

While the academic analysis at the time of the plane's design provided confidence that its proposed performance could be met, the plane demonstrated both favorable and unfavorable characteristics once it was actually flown. New aircraft always have unexpected features when they pass from the design stage to actual practice. In the P-38's case, what was not expected from the original proposal data was the plane's unusual degree of refinement in detail design and construction. For instance, all its external surfaces were smooth with no disturbances from rivets or lap joints of the skin. To maintain a precise contour of the external surface, the internal structure was adjusted by a few thousandths of an inch to compensate for varying skin thickness and butt joints.

The initial P-38 suffered from two serious bugs. On its first flight, flap flutter developed in the takeoff setting of the flaps with an accompanying wing flutter.* Correction involved both minor structural changes and aerodynamic investigation and modification. Wind-tunnel investigation showed that the airflow between the leading edge of the flap and the cavity into which it retracted was restricted, and an unsteady flow resulted.

Instead of redesigning the wing structure or the flap, Kelly Johnson followed a precept attributed to William B. Stout, builder of the Ford Tri-motor: "Simplicate and add more lightness." Johnson cut holes in the cavity lining, which eased the air flow around the leading edge of the flaps as they extended out and back.

A second, relatively simple bug took more time and effort. Initially, the wheel brakes proved to be incapable of absorbing the energy of the heavy plane at high ground speeds. New wheels and brakes had to be designed and built.

Because of the P-38's weight and clean design, its dive speeds at high altitude were unusually fast. The plane introduced us to "compressibility," the dynamic changes in airflow and flight characteristics that occur when a plane approaches the speed of sound. This involved severe buffeting, loss of control, and nonrecoverable vertical dives until lower altitudes and higher temperatures were reached. The exploration was hazardous, and the interim solutions were not easily found. But continued investigation provided basic knowledge that had universal application to all subsequent high-speed flight.

The plane always suffered from the psychological appraisal that it was "too large for a fighter." Although the performance more than met estimates and the pilots who learned to exploit its superior characteristics found its maneuverability adequate, many specific objections related primarily to its size. The Republic P-47 suffered somewhat from the same problem, and it was finally called a fighter bomber to reconcile the psychological conflict.

This evaluation process merely backtracks the logic used by design engineers in

---

* EDITOR'S NOTE: The first flight of the P-38 was made by the author.

arriving at final composite configurations. In addition, it is duplicated in the analysis of the structural design to substantiate weight and producibility factors. And in a somewhat similar fashion, performance estimates are traced back to the basic assumptions of lift, drag, and propulsive efficiency. This entire effort is aimed at establishing a credibility and confidence rating. Although this seems elemental, many people wrongly think that bid figures are compared against each other for relative standing and that all pertinent material is presented in the bid data without much chance of discriminating between the honest and the unscrupulous proposal. In the last anaylsis, the only distinction between two authentic and sound proposals may lie in the subtle differentiation in a single confidence factor. All this selection process assumes extraordinary importance during periods when funding or manufacturing facilities are scarce, such as the mid-1930s when funding was low.

THREE STAGES OF DEVELOPMENT

Regardless of the procurement form, there were always three distinct stages of development that merited protecting. First, there was the experimental article for each category—for instance, bombers or fighters. This could result from a negotiated purchase, a design competition, or a change order. This article would represent a potential quantity production some two to four years in the future. Next, the service test stage was as much a development level as a part of procurement. And finally, the production stage of quantity production was the end result of development and was, in the late 1930s, the "physical article competition" form of contract.

In an *idealized* state, the three stages would, in staggered generations, simultaneously represent progressive state of the art. At the experimental level, some models would be selected for advancement to the service test category, where the problems of going from prototype to limited production would be worked out and operational suitability would be more fully evaluated. From the service test articles, selections would be made for quantity production. The production stage would provide insurance for expanded production in an emergency.

This progression from experimental plane to quantity production would maximize technical progress and provide the best capability for equipping an expanding combat force with modern aircraft in an emergency. This ideal format presupposes

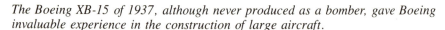

The Boeing XB-15 of 1937, although never produced as a bomber, gave Boeing invaluable experience in the construction of large aircraft.

118

that all types of planes, both bombers and fighters, could follow concurrent programs. Such a complete plan was obviously infeasible in the period before World War II.

One conclusion that might be drawn from the records is that the design competition process did not result in producing significantly better potential types for production in the emergency. This process was just one way of achieving progress, and it must be recognized that it never was possible to follow an orderly procedure step-by-step from initial conception to final production of quantities for the inventory. If each ad hoc procedure contributed some little bit to the overall accomplishment, it must be recognized as a successful expedient, although it may seem transient in retrospect.

For instance, the four classified and restricted competitions that resulted in the XB-15, the XB-19, the XP-38, and the XP-39 illustrate in differing ways how the contributions may be both direct and indirect. The fact that the XB-15 provided the basis for the B-17 is well recognized, although the only *direct* spin-off from the effort was the Boeing 314 flying boat. The XB-19 provided much detailed development and a necessary element of confidence that large airplanes were feasible, even though the XB-19 itself was not produced. The later B-36 was substantially the same size as the 19 and probably would not have been attempted if the XB-19 had not broken the trail some years earlier. The original Douglas DC-4, and later the C-54, undoubtedly benefited from the design and construction experience gained in the XB-19 project. The XP-39, originally with a turbosupercharger, which was later eliminated, led to a production type, although it fell short of the projected performance that had been only a long-shot possibility when the competition was conceived. The XP-38 demonstrated its potential, and by using first the service test negotiated procedure and later the authority provided in the expansion procurement, it went on to be a significant factor in the war.

CHANGE ORDERS

One of the more useful forms of negotiated contract was the change order to an existing contract. Because of the budget and appropriation process, the justification for a new experimental program must be prepared almost two years before a competition can be held. Not only are the type specification characteristics for an

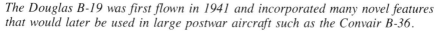

The Douglas B-19 was first flown in 1941 and incorporated many novel features that would later be used in large postwar aircraft such as the Convair B-36.

airplane that will not be built for another two or more years somewhat indefinite, but authorities who must approve the money find it difficult to recognize or justify the need. Consequently, any project that can utilize already available funds for at least part of its cost saves a couple of years and a lot of argument. Besides, the short lines of communications and the close working relationships between the services and the industry made the change order an expeditious procedure.

Change orders range all the way from minor structural modifications with no resulting change in cost or performance to major configuration and power changes. Manufacturing and early service experience dictate mandatory and desirable alterations so that some evolutionary process goes on even in series production of a relatively fixed design. The World War II experience divided these alterations into block changes that resulted not only in new letter-suffix designations but also in numerical series changes within letter-suffix groups. In wartime, this process became imperative and general, but though it had been less extensive in peacetime, a precedent had been recognized and developed. This maintained the high production rates that kept wartime types of aircraft competitive in combat. Although supply and logistics were inevitably made more difficult by modifications and changes, the life span of planes in combat was short, and the earlier models dropped out shortly. In the last analysis, superiority in combat was the overriding consideration.

Not all the experimental articles resulting from change orders were eminently successful as production prototypes. They did influence progress, however. When the YB-17 static test article was converted by a change order to a flying article, it included the turbosupercharger for high-altitude performance and actually became the prototype configuration for subsequent production planes. The XP-37, which was an effort to use a supercharger in what was originally a P-36, did go into a service test quantity, but the rear pilot position needed for balance with the supercharger and intercooler in front was considered unsuitable in operation. It did serve to confirm the contention that the small fighter type needed to have higher power and higher altitude ratings built into its engines. The P-43, a sort of intermediate type of plane in the procurement process, solved the supercharger weight and balance problem by putting the supercharger aft, a configuration that was followed in the P-47. The XP-40, which was the flying prototype for a sample article competition for quantity production, through subsequent modifications became the wartime aircraft that was used so extensively.

Aside from the change order for experimental models, there were variations that extended the life and utility of types already adopted. The B-18A utilized both the later developments of the DC-3 commercial planes and operational-utility modifications resulting from service experience, as was evidenced by its different nose and bombardier-gunner accommodations. The B-23, which was a revision of the last B18s, would have provided the basis for quantity production but its timing missed the surge for quantity that developed with the emergency.

The procurement of speculative and proprietary articles was clearly within the permissive prerogatives that the 1926 law gave to the secretary of war. While the process did provide stimulus for subsequent development, it did not provide a notable entry point for procurement. It indicated one way of avoiding the unsatisfactory features of sole-source procurement from design proposals, which was always suspect and generally avoided. During one extended period, Howard Hughes asked for a sole-source contract to develop a fighter from his very successful racer. Although his small engineering and construction staff obviously could have built a single good military plane, there was no guarantee that it would have been better than one built on the same basis by one of the other established builders with complete manufacturing capability. Hughes was urged to build a plane on specula-

Winner of the 1936 pursuit competition, the Seversky P-35 evolved into the P-43 and famous Republic P-47 Thunderbolt.

The Douglas B-23 Dragon, whose production was quite limited, was used during the war for training, coastal patrol, and glider tow duty.

tion to demonstrate the ability, and there was every likelihood that it could have been bought, at least for experimental purposes. But he elected not to do this. He was always included in requestor bids, but his proposals did not win in competition with other designs. However, the speculative channel was open.

The type specifications that were used for procurement were never ad hoc creations devised for the particular procurement. Tentative specifications were continually revised, even if they were not used, and the one chosen at the appropriate time was always an evolutionary development. The revisions continually reflected changes in the state of the art and in engine development, as well as in the operational desires for armament or equipment. They were used for tentatively approving reviewing agencies and service representatives from operational units to keep operational concepts up to date, even though no procurement was possible. They also kept steady the progression of design studies and the translation of states of the art into preliminary combat-suitable designs.

THE PROCUREMENT PROCESS

In all the detailed historical research and in the record, little notice is made of one group whose activity was essential and whose efforts are rarely given due credit. These were the procurement and legal officers and the civilian specialists who worked together in the headquarters. They were always caught between the operational needs of the service, usually expressed very strongly by sincere and vigorous people, and the higher levels of the Army, the Navy, the secretary's office, and Congress. Regulations and procedures were continually devised and revised, and most were rejected. It was frustrating, but the best that could be done usually fell far short of what the operators wanted.

The volume of data that was sent out with each request for a bid has often been noted. The material supposedly needed to define in detail all the terms of competitive bidding, and as has also been noted, it had to serve both the experienced manufacturer and the first-time competitor. The data that went out, of course, generated an equally impressive volume of information submitted by the bidder. But in addition to these unavoidable paper mills, the procurement staffs had to prepare equally voluminous in-house documentation that described the preparation of each form and document going out to prospective bidders and the methods for handling all of the data that was expected to come in. The preparation of the final reports and the form of submission for review were covered by regulations and procedural documents. Although these internal data did not get outside the service, their preparation was time consuming. Each change in procedure or interpretation of the laws or regulations required changes in all of this.

One factor always intervened to upset planning. This was the large increment of engineering required to go from any one model of a type to another. As noted by Kindelberger in his 1948 testimony, the engineering of a new type of aircraft is *never* complete, no matter how far along the plane may be in production. There was always the expectation in "outside" circles that once one plane had been built following a new basic design, subsequent aircraft were mere reproductions. Some sample checks by Wright Field project officers in the 1930s indicate that going from an already existing prototype to the next step in limited production absorbed about as much engineering as preparing the original design had.

A simple illustration explains why this was so. In order to maintain an efficient weight-to-strength relationship, the assumed, or measured, loads must be chased through each piece of material, bolt, and fitting and then distributed to adjacent parts 122 in what is called a stress analysis in a time-consuming, meticulous process. A relatively minor change—regardless of whether it is meant to facilitate quantity production, to correct unanticipated difficulties, to improve combat suitability (such as by adding another gun or more bombs), or to take advantage of an improved engine model to increase performance—requires not only the detail design of the mounting or attaching fittings but also the redistribution of the concentrated loads into the original structure. A small increase in gross weight, another gun, or some more ammunition, may, for instance, require redesign of the wing root attachments. A change that affects performance may mean redistributing the aerodynamic loads on even remote parts. For example, more power may mean reinforcing the tail.

There is no provision in the budget process for contingency funding, since it can become an unallocated grab bag. The total figures in different government departments for any year are pretty well determined by political and overall economic estimates. The details have to be specifically justified, although there is recognition that they are imprecise. Reprogramming within the totals takes care of rates of expenditure that differ from the original estimates and of priorities that change with time. During the 1930s, each year's appropriation had to be rejustified in detail, which added another sticky complication to problems such as the big bombers that took several years of funding to complete.

Fortunately, the war emergency expedited appropriation procedures to take care of many of the problems that arose with the planes needed in quantity for combat. Although there is probably no breakdown of expenses that can be analyzed, the costs involved in taking the B-17 from a 34,000-pound prototype to a 64,000-pound final combat model undoubtedly exceeded by many times the original model's engineering costs. In fact, just the addition of turrets and some of the increases in power probably exceeded the original design costs. Certainly, such cases as the unexpected compressibility effects that were met in the YP-38 because it reached previously unattainable speeds involved costs for investigation and correction that must have been higher than the prototypes' total original engineering and testing costs.

Underlying all discussion of procurement procedures and difficulties is the conclusion that success depended upon the experience and dedication of a small number of people, both in industry and the services, who were involved in the nuts and bolts of the business and who were largely unrecognized but whose efforts were essential in the attainment of the final products. Fortunately, in the engineering and procurement functions of the services, military officers normally served multiple tours in related jobs so that their experience was utilized. Many civilians served for their entire active careers in a specialized field, such as engineering. In industry, the established companies always had an advantage because of their cadres of experienced and clever people. The smaller outfits, which seemed to have technical capabilities that would have been desirable to exploit, were deficient in functions that seemed to be purely administrative but were so essential. As a result, retired or resigned military personnel frequently found opportunities with the manufacturers. It took the combined ingenuity and cooperation of the industry and the government procurement agencies to make the system work.

VII THE PEOPLE AND THEIR PLANES

In the battle of Crécy in 1346, English bowmen armed with longbows defeated a French force of mounted knights in armor. Since then, historians have commonly argued that the battle demonstrated the superiority of the longbow over mounted armor. But in claiming this, they have missed other factors that were really significant. When considered more fully, the character of the forces and the quality of leadership were probably more decisive than the weapons. Designating the Black Prince, Edward, as the hero may have been a more timely and accurate appraisal. The inseparability of human elements in the employment of arms was demonstrated here, as it has been all through history.

The English force was composed of free men, though they were probably more nearly conscripts than volunteers. They were, however, neither professional military types nor representatives of the English elite. Their background included a degree of independence tempered by respect for authority. The French were, on the other hand, a collection of privileged and formal groups. They had their own petty loyalties and rivalries and were encumbered by rigid traditions.

The English leadership and chain of command were obviously superior in refusing battle until a suitable site had been selected and then in distributing their force and committing it advantageously. The French force, due to its fragmented nature, apparently was unable to mount a concerted effort. Commanding it must have been tedious and difficult.

It might be concluded that free men make better soldiers than professionals or mercenaries do. This is not unlike natives or Indians ambushing superior troops armed with more sophisticated weapons. Similarly, a strong case can be made that the differences in command and command structure were important to the battle's result. The selection of site is a command function, but the geography itself may be considered of paramount importance. The piecemeal commitment of the French force violated the simplest principle of combat. Although it had epic historical significance, the use of gunpowder by the English for the first time probably did not influence the outcome.

Considering the total array of contributing factors, the relative merits of bows and arrows versus spears and swords seem unimportant. If the arms at Crécy had been different, the battle would have been fought differently and perhaps not even at the same exact spot. But it is reasonable to suppose that the French would have been defeated even if the English had been armed with nothing but rocks.

PEOPLE AND AERIAL COMBAT

In aerial combat, the same considerations apply. The best airplane is the one with the best pilot or crew; the best design is the one with the best designers and builders. In either case, skill is part of what makes a person be the best at a task, and training is another part. But they are only *small* parts of the whole. The dedication, ingenuity, and courage, in the broadest sense, of the people involved are the most influential factors.

The relative rating of aircraft in combat is strongly influenced by the disposition and employment of forces, as determined by command decisions. In this respect, aircraft successful in one theater might be unsuccessful in another. This is no different than the situation in Crécy six centuries ago. For instance, the Me-262, which would have to be rated as a superior individual fighter, was committed by Hitler to low-level strike missions. Here, its advantages were degraded. Employed in air-to-air combat, its natural element, it was nevertheless dominated by overwhelming superior numbers of allied fighters.

What was called the numbers racket, an expression used to deplore the apparent sacrifice of quality in favor of quantity production in the early stages of the war build-up, was merely another difficult command decision made at the highest level. It permitted theater command decisions that concentrated forces in critical engagements. Whether the subject is operations, command, strategy, or manufacture, the airplane cannot be evaluated or appreciated as an example of sophisticated weaponry without full consideration of the roles played by the people involved.

A review of record-breaking performances, racing events, and other newsworthy items during the 1920s and 1930s reveals that familiar names kept reappearing. It was natural with so few people involved that whenever something of note occurred, there had to be some thread of relationship throughout the existing fabric.

This held true both in the military and in civilian circles. Throughout this period, individuals in many facets of aviation—administrators, commanders, engineers, manufacturers—were still active pilots; and many of them had outstanding performances to their credit. While many were recognized for outstanding flying or for superior ability demonstrated in nonflying positions of responsibility, several men enjoyed this combination of experience at all levels.

Gen. Hap Arnold's career reflected this broad and varied experience to a remarkable degree. As commander of the Army Air Forces, he held as high and responsible a position as could be attained. When he was a wing commander at March Field in the early 1930s, it would have been considered unremarkable that he trained with the Wrights at the beginning of miliary flying in the United States. No pilot flying airmail in the West when the Air Corps was given the job from February to June, 1934, would have thought much about the fact that the commander of the Western Division, Arnold, had held a series of responsible positions during World War I. When later in 1934, he led a formation flight of the new B-10s on a flight to Alaska to demonstrate the new potential for rapid deployment to this outpost, he was simply reverting to active flier status. For this, he received the MacKay Trophy for the second time. Incidentally, at this time he was still a lieutenant colonel; the Air Corps was still a young man's game. In 1938, when he became chief of Air Corps, his past tours at the Industrial College and with the Field Service Section of the Materiel Division undoubtedly helped him make difficult decisions concerning procurement and manufacture.

While General Arnold represents the epitome of broad and varied experience, individuals at all levels of the military were exposed to similar experience. This led to general acceptance of others on the basis of current activity, with little regard to past performance. To an unexpected degree, it was supposed that everyone was qualified for a job at hand, and rank or position was of less importance than ability to perform.

Ralph Damon represents the same sort of mobility in moving from one position of responsibility to another within the civilain aviation field. He went to work with 125

Curtiss after learning to fly during World War I and serving in the Air Corps until 1922. Moving up in the manufacturing side of the business, he went to St. Louis as factory manager when this division of the company was established. When Curtiss was revitalizing its military programs, he was made president of the Curtiss-Wright Airplane Company. Then, in 1936, he went to American Airlines as its vice president for operations. When Republic Aviation was faced with the problems of expanded production in 1941, he was induced to take leave from American Airlines and become Republic's president. In 1943, he returned to American, and two years later became its president. Four years later, he joined TWA as president.

Not all individuals who had exceptionally broad experience or who established records were pilots, company presidents, or commanders. There was Don Young. When Roscoe Turner won the Thompson Trophy race for the third time in 1939, he brought Young with him to receive the trophy. Turner said something to the effect that he owed his life to Young, who, as his mechanic for years, had done all the delicate work to keep the racing machines at top performance. In addition, Young had supervised the construction of the different racers at Wedell-Williams and at Matty Laird's. He was one of those ubiquitous characters who were part engineer, part manufacturing superintendent, and part super-mechanic who combined skill with uncanny judgment. When the first P-38s came out, Don Young was there, working for Lockheed and helping to shepherd the new planes and pilots through the growing pains associated with a new and unfamiliar type.

THE ERA OF NEW RESPONSIBILITIES

With the expansion of air activity at the end of the 1930s, it was inevitable that most of the individuals who had been engaged in the various earlier phases found themselves rapidly moved up to positions of ever-increasing responsiblity. The natural result was that all during World War II whenever any group was assembled, there were several men present who had had some common experience. Surprisingly, many of these experiences involved being participants in some flying event or active operational service. While there were many aviators who had remained in the active service since World War I, there were others who had returned to civilian life in the interim but came back into the service and served with distinction.

Frank O. D. ("Monk") Hunter had been a distinguished fighter pilot in World War I. He appeared in various command positions and was a member of some of the boards and committees that influenced the direction of development and the selection of types in the mid-1930s. When the First Pursuit Group was deployed by air in P-38s across the North Atlantic to England in 1942, he led it as commanding general of the Eighth Fighter Command.

Edward P. Curtis ended World War I as a major and an ace. After moving through the hierarchy of the Kodak company, he rejoined the Air Corps as a major in World War II. He became a major general and served as executive officer to General Spaatz, who commanded the Strategic Air Forces in England. Curtis's influence was substantial, and after the war, President Dwight Eisenhower selected him to be an adviser on aviation matters. (Incidentally, he and another pilot accepted the surrender of a German pilot with a Fokker D. VII that eventually was placed on exhibit in the Smithsonian Institution.)

At the beginning of World War II, as in World War I, the training requirements to meet the demands of units being organized and of planes being built exceeded the capacity of military peacetime schools. Similarly, civilian training capacity had to be utilized to meet the challenge. In World War I, many of the early fliers before 1917 had found their services invaluable as the nucleus for instructor training. The record, from 1938 on, of civilian schools for pilots and mechanics makes a complete history in itself. It is sufficient here to recognize that the civilian aviation community that had had such a struggle to survive during the Depression served as an essential element in the establishment of air power and ultimate victory.

Hundreds of boards and committees were formed throughout the 1920s and 1930s to review every facet of aviation and the military. There were boards to establish requirements and characteristics of aircraft. There were evaluation boards to make selections for procurement. Then, there were committees established by Congress or the president or by the secretaries of war or the navy. Although it is difficult to determine just what impact each had, their reiteration of the inadequacy of America's defense and aircraft capability must have had some cumulative effect.

A listing of the personnel who were active in these review functions and in the administration of key organizations such as the NACA, Manufacturers Aircraft Association (later, the Aircraft Industries Association), the CAA, and the Aeronautical Chamber of Commerce reveals the same predominance of names that were well known in the aviation world. Except for Lindbergh, very few of these people excited enough outside attention to warrant biographies. After the war, historians and biographers began to recognize some of the more colorful figures. Generals Arnold, Doolittle, and Ira C. Eaker became well known.

It has been noted that, because of the short history of aviation up to 1940, many active participants in the preamble to World War II were in at the beginning of aircraft development. Grover Loening worked with the Wrights as an engineer and had a profound effect all during his life. General Foulois took the Army's first Wright pusher to Fort Sam Houston at San Antonio and taught himself to fly with correspondence help from Wilbur Wright. He became chief of Air Corps in 1931 and served in that capacity until 1934. During this period, he waged a continuing struggle with the general staff and the politicians to get recognition of air power's growing potential. His efforts undoubtedly laid the ground work for the later acceptance of the concept of an independent air force.

PEOPLE AND PLANES

The impact of individuals upon planes and their effectiveness is difficult to appraise in detail. Engineers such as Welwood Beall of Boeing, Arthur Raymond of Douglas, Kelly Johnson of Lockheed, and Don Berlin of Curtiss definitely put their stamp on their companies' products. Then, there were such individuals as Reuben Fleet, Dutch Kindelberger, Leroy Grumman, and Chance M. Vought who established their own companies. The commanders of the Army and Navy air arms profoundly affected all aspects of organization, operational doctrine, and procurement.

The effectiveness of combat aircraft depended on the understanding and ability of the pilots to exploit the inherent characteristics of the type of plane they were flying. Anthony W. LeVier was a successful racing pilot in the 1930s. He became a test pilot at Lockheed. But his most valuable contributions were made in visiting combat groups, demonstrating maximum-performance tactics, and helping pilots to become more effective. James Mattern, another noted figure in long-distance flights, did the same thing using a modified two-seater P-38. During the 1930s, one of the functions of Materiel Division project officers was to go to the operating units when new types were first introduced to demonstrate preferred operating techniques.

One of the most difficult problems for pilots and crews newly introduced to combat was to recognize that the performance of any plane was less significant than its employment. Bombers that strayed from the mutual fire support of their companions were targets for attack by the enemy. It would have been impossible to provide 127 enough defensive fire power for one airplane to stand off a concerted attack. There were frequent complaints that a particular fighter had inadequate climb and acceleration to counter an enemy attacking from above. The realization that surprise attack from a superior position could not be countered by performance alone had to be acquired rapidly. Conversely, combat stressed the importance of utilizing these same factors to a degree that was never realized in training.

Technical development strove always to provide competitive performance, but clear superiority was never attainable by technical means alone. Two veterans of the Battle of Britain, Robert Stanford-Tuck and Adolph Gysbert ("Sailor") Malan, came to the United States to help indoctrinate our fighter pilots. They also flew our fighters in competition with our unit and test pilots. They used position, maneuver, and the sun so instinctively that it made little difference what airplane they flew. Their performances were always superb.

There were gunners and fighter pilots who fired such long bursts that the overheated barrels of their guns destroyed their accuracy. Some of the better shots always seemed to have ammunition left, while others consistently ran out of ammunition. The difference in attainable range varied in operating units by as much as 15 percent. Techniques for conserving fuel and increasing range were matters for continual indoctrination in all theaters. It took a long time to recognize that the technical performance figures simply measured engineering characteristics and not operational figures. While useful for comparative purposes, they were frequently misleading. Airplanes in combat were never at a standard weight or at any one altitude. They were operated at varying power settings, and the amount of ammunition or fuel that they needed depended on whether or how long they had been engaged in combat.

In peace as well as in combat, the same airplane could be given a high rating by one evaluator and a low rating by another equally conscientious evaluator. This stemmed from the dual nature of a military aircraft. It was simultaneously a weapon and a vehicle.

During the peacetime period when the aircraft were developed, the probable suitability of the complete system of plane, equipment, and crew had to be assumed. The handling and performance of the article as a vehicle could be judged in the abstract, but under the pressures and restrictions of combat, these characteristic were ambiguous, at best. An airplane with adequate armament provisions, ease of loading, good bombardier station, and superior vision might be considered excellent, even if its handling and performance were marginal. The B-26 was rated well in combat, but in training and as a vehicle, it acquired a poor reputation. On the other hand, there were pilots who would accept marginal armament provisions if the takeoff, landing, handling, and maneuver promised to let them get the most from the craft. Vision and instrument flying characteristics might thus be more critical than maximum performance figures.

It is hard to imagine, in view of its combat record, that the B-17 was welcomed and deplored at the same time. When it first appeared, it was the first example of the potentially heavy bomber that had been wanted for so long. The first service test planes were treated with great respect and established an outstanding record. They fully justified the hopes of their supporters. However, the British had a few of them and were not impressed. For those who had sights set on truly long-range heavy-load bombers, the service test B-17s represented only a preliminary step. So the next larger version was initiated almost before the B-17s came into service. These were the B-29s. But even these were not big enough. For transoceanic range, or rather radius, a larger size was needed. Thus, the B-36.

The B-15 had broken trail for the B-29, and the B-19 had shown that the 4000-

A sleek and powerful machine, the Martin B-26 Marauder was the mainstay of the American medium-bomber force in Europe during World War II.

Based on lessons learned flying earlier models in combat, the Boeing B-17E featured a redesigned fuselage and other modifications.

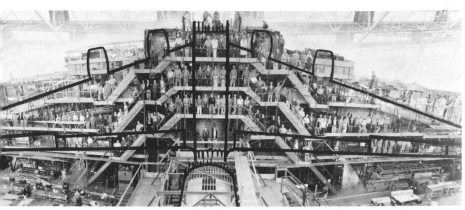

This photo graphically illustrates the wing size of the Douglas B-19.

129

square-foot wing-area machine was feasible.

The evaluation of an aircraft is never quite objective, and it is always possible to get widely divergent views. Both positive and negative reports can be correct if they are considered in light of the appraisers' viewpoints. But the critical element is that the people are as important as the plane.

When the P-26A first appeared in 1934, it represented the first transitional aircraft replacing the old stick-and-wire biplanes. It was an all-metal monoplane, but it was thin winged and required external wire bracing. It had a fixed landing gear and an open cockpit. Nevertheless, it had better high speed, climb, and generally desirable performance than its predecessors had. But along with higher wing loading and a correspondingly higher speed in maneuver, the P-26A also had a larger turning radius; in turning competition, the older, slower planes could turn inside and close up to firing range. Until its superior climb and speed were used to advantage with its better acceleration, the P-26A was rated as inferior in simulated combat.

The P-26A did have a higher landing speed, and with its narrow landing gear and soft shock struts, it tended to be tricky on the ground. Some of the adverse comments were so severe that they rated the machine unserviceable.

In reviewing the acceptance board proceedings to find out why the plane had been accepted, it was discovered that the board had considered high speed to be of paramount importance and had been willing to accept undesirable characteristics to obtain it. When the relatively high landing speed was pointed out as perhaps affecting the utility adversely, the reply was that the pilots could learn to adapt.

Early in the P-26A's service, the differences in maneuver characteristics tended to assume lesser importance. But the takeoff and landing characteristics remained unsatisfactory. Flaps were added to the plane in a retrofit program. After a while, it was found that the pilots considered the flaps unnecessary and preferred landing without using them. The merry-go-round had been completed, and the P-26A became the new standard. Any attempt to get an objective rating of the suitability of the plane would have depended entirely upon the stage at which the evaluation was made.

EVALUATION OF THE AIRCRAFT

The evaluations that people make of planes determine their acceptance and the uses to which they are put. Airplanes, yachts, machine tools, and earth-moving machinery suffer from a common ailment. Operators and owners always feel that if the next larger size could be afforded, it would have enough greater capability to do some of the jobs they would like to do much more effectively or quickly. With airplanes, it is the next degree of sophisticated equipment, or a little more range, or a little more power, or speed, or armament.

This characteristic is neither superficial nor casual when it comes to setting requirements or deciding procurements. What is worse, it is never settled and continues through time. It gives rise to serious criticism that in many cases is unfounded. The basic truth is that an armed force is not limited to the one article under consideration, but it requires all sizes in some numerical balance.

The key concern is what is affordable. A large military airplane costs roughly three times as much as one that is half its size. So one of the balancing factors is whether three small aircraft can do more than one large plane. This leads to the numbers racket, which can be very efficient—particularly when the smaller plane can be obtained quickly and the larger one may take longer. Further, one article can only be in one place at any time. When deployment or dispersion to various areas of combat is a serious consideration, the value of having more planes is considerable.

This has to be balanced against combat suitability.

The period of near stagnation in the 1930s tended to intensify this ambiguity. There was always a desire to get the largest article, on the one hand, and to get the smallest light-weight fighter, on the other. When money availability is restricted, the desire to get the smaller solution is intensified, as military planners hope that desired performances can be obtained by some kind of magic. Technology, unfortunately, dictates possibilities. Money shortages also make it difficult to face the necessity of providing planes in graded sizes so that a truly balanced force can be had.

Procurement rules and regulations together with their various interpretations supposedly eliminated, or reduced, the impact of individuals in the process in the 1930s. But since priority rankings were never explicitly stated for quantity, performance, and timeliness when procurement goals were set, the forms of competitive procurement tended to be restrictive or subject to misinterpretation. In fact, the basic factors of competition for procurement are both advantageous and disadvantageous in varying degrees. Balancing them involves compromise and careful judgment. Having many planes provides for the existence of a force in being and has appeal both to politicians and planners. But short of an emergency, the rate of replacement with improved types is also of paramount importance. Large-quantities at one time causes gaps in replacement and can lead to a preponderantly obsolete force with less than competitive performance. Cost of units is at times an overwhelming consideration, depending as it does on economic and political factors beyond the scope of defense considerations. While low cost tends to support the maintenance of an adequate force, it also tends to compromise quality. The pursuit of perfection or outstanding performance, though desirable, can price a proposed aircraft out of realistic attainability, delay its development, or reduce the number of planes built.

These factors affecting the choice and funding of all military weapons, including aircraft, are timeless and were not unique to the 1930s. The general shortage of total funding during the period did have the impact of demanding decisions that were not always desirable.

There is always a futile hope, or illusion, that some particular law or regulation will automatically suppress all disadvantages and simultaneously ensure superior products. Some requirements impose such a burden on industrial competitors that they raise objections that bias the selections or are forced out of competition. The B-17 situation has been cited to illustrate this point.

All that can be concluded is, first, that it should be expected that *no* one procedure will fit all situations and second, that people will interpret and utilize *all* provisions of the law in different ways. If enough people are ingenious, daring, and persevering, they can find solutions within the established rules. To a remarkable degree, people in all areas of the aviation activity were successful in adapting to the situation before World War II. Certainly, the period of the 1930s contained many examples of conflicts, adaptations, and multiple approaches to achieve at least a potential capability of providing the base for the air power that eventually was needed.

The 1926 act defined competition and provided enough flexibility for the secretaries of war and the Navy and the development/procurement agencies to make as much headway as money would allow. By 1934–35, some aspects of Army procurement reinforced by competitive pressures from a struggling industry brought about political and public questioning. The counter was the "prototype physical article" competition for Air Corps production, combined with a numerical determination of "figures of merit" and final "points per dollar" during the evaluation process. This satisfied Congress and worked quite well. We were never forced to buy whatever was the cheapest, and, in general, got the best.

In an attempt to produce a lightweight fighter from non-strategic materials, the Bell Aircraft Company designed the diminutive XP-77.

The Navy, on the other hand, never quite agreed with a numerical determination of quality, which seemed to its officials to be judgment matter. Its procurement stuck with the design competition provisions of the old act. This process found winner aircraft, but it required an extra step to get a manufacturing source. A few instances of selecting a production source other than the original designer led to difficulties; so the normal routine became negotiating with the design winner for production. The differences between the two services developed from outside influences and the differing philosophies of the responsible individuals involved.

The Air Corps and the secretary of war continued to use design competitions and negotiated procurement of service test articles where it was advantageous. In short, *all* the allowable procedures were exploited when necessary. Proprietary prototypes created even in the absence of a formal requirement were almost universally procured on a sole-source negotiated basis. Having designers build models of aircraft for testing identified the creators as the responsible sources and met legal requirements, if it was determined to be in the best interests of the service.

At one time the cliché "4,000 pounds, 400 horsepower, 400 miles per hour" represented the hope for a small, inexpensive solution to the fighter requirement. General Arnold wanted the Caudron race plane of the 1938 races examined to determine whether what appeared to be advanced technology could be used to obtain a usable pursuit plane. When allowances were made for armament, minimum tactical range, maintenance features, wheels for service use, instruments, and vision, the technological requirements almost exactly matched the specification figures for the P-36, which we already had. However, the continued interest in the possibility led, apparently, to the experimental XP-77, the small wooden plane built by Bell that never exhibited much promise.

If there is any hope of resolving this dilemma in the future, it lies in keeping adequate separation between sizes to avoid proliferation of types of aircraft with overlapping capabilities. The pressures of war tend to force this kind of solution. Recognizing it is quite hard, however, and planning for it is much more difficult still.

When the aircraft used in World War II were in the planning stages, there was no distinct plan for where they would be used, if ever. There was some guidance in intelligence reports, which indicated what performance was needed to be competitive. Certainly, there was little to suggest a thousand bomber plane raids, even though "mass bombing" was a vague concept. The speed and altitude requirements were largely intended to make interception difficult. It is doubtful that serious consideration would have been given to forecasts of the possibility of carpets of anti-aircraft fire, as were encountered over Germany. In Europe, the B-24s were more vulnerable because they had to fly 2,000 to 4,000 feet lower than the B-17s flew.

A qualitative evaluation of these two planes, based on performance and configuration, would have suggested that the B-24 might be a better all-round bomber with superior altitude and speed. However, the B-24 at high altitude "wallowed" when it carried a load. Different characteristics of the automatic pilot might have corrected this. The operational engineering section of the Eighth Air Force in England experimented with a ventral fin that was intended primarily to protect the tail of the fuselage on the ground when aft loading tipped the plane backward. It did, incidentally, improve directional damping at high altitude and promised the possibility of flying satisfactorily at somewhat increased altitudes. Although the evidence was not

Though sometimes overshadowed by B-17 exploits in Europe, the Consolidated B-24 Liberator was the mainstay in the Pacific until the advent of the Boeing B-29.

conclusive, it is intriguing that an improvement in auto-pilot characteristics or the addition of three or four square feet of fin surface might have had as much beneficial effect as adding some 10 percent more power and thereby changing the plane's acceptance rating.

P-38s in Alaska and the Pacific operated over long distances before they met enemy counteraction. In Europe, the aircraft were destined to accompany bombers on their deepest penetrations over defended enemy territory. The enemy certainly knew that the fighters had been ferried across the ocean and were capable of long-range flights. If the P-38s could be forced to fight on the way into German-held areas, they would have to drop auxiliary fuel tanks and expend ammunition, leaving the bombers without protection from the target on their way out. As a result, the P-38s were the preferred targets for German fighters until the P-51s, which had 133 extended ranges, arrived to take over the load. This tended to discourage the P-38 pilots.

The Allison engine seemed to behave poorly with the aromatic fuels in England. Although the compressibility dive problems were not frequently encountered in combat, and although Cass S. Hough had demonstrated that recovery was possible after lower altitudes were reached, these two factors further reduced enthusiasm.

When the First Pursuit Group arrived in England and was preparing for its first combat missions, Harry Broadhust (later air chief marshall) visited the station to give the pilots some pointers on what to expect. He had been in the United States at the same time as Stanford-Tuck and Malan and had flown all our planes competitively. He mentioned that the P-38 had performed quite well when flown by the American project officer but that he would personally prefer to be in a Spit. This was taken by the new pilots to mean that the P-38 might not stand up to the Germans.

Taken altogether, the P-38 did very well in all theaters with outstanding scores and survival rates. But in the United Kingdom, it was less successful. Certainly, the attitude with which it was operated suffered from these factors, which were psychological but very real. None of these could have been cranked into the considerations

Colonels Cass Hough and Ben Kelsey stand in front of a Lockheed P-38 Lightning. Kelsey commanded the Operational Engineering Section of the U.S. Eighth Air Force in England during World War II.

Built as a refinement of the P-26, the Boeing XP-940 featured an enclosed cockpit, a fully cantilevered wing, and a semi-retractable landing gear.

associated with the initial conception or evaluation of the aircraft. People have to operate the planes, and the performance of people is as critical as the performance of the weapon.

When P-51 fighters accompanied B-17 bombers on the shuttle flight from bases in East Anglia to Piryatin and Poltava in Russia, they demonstrated a number of significant points that had been developing over the years. It was expected that the big bombers could make the long flight of some 1,300 miles, but that the fighters could make their presence felt at these distances seemed revolutionary. It should not have been surprising, however, since missions had earlier been run to the Polish border and back to England.

It had been known for years that the range of airplanes depended only on their efficiency and not on their size. There was extra strength built into fighters for violent maneuver. To fly long-range, they had to be overloaded so that the weight of fuel became the same percentage of gross weight as it was for a long-range airplane. Since this overload amounted to as much as 25 percent of the design gross weight, there had to be enough power to permit takeoff and about the same maneuverability while heavily loaded as a bomber might have.

In the 1920s and early 1930s, it had been standard to use belly tanks for fighters and to carry them on attachments that might alternately be used for light-bomb racks. With the P-26, it was decreed that auxiliary fuel (overload above the design weight) should be carried in internal tanks to reduce drag. This concept was carried into the later monoplanes with the added admonition that no external fuel tanks would be carried on fighters with retractable landing gears to reduce the risk of fire in inadvertent wheels-up landings.

Although there were prohibitions against external fuel tanks and against bomb racks for fighters, the concept of extra fuel for extending range had never been lost in this country. This was largely due to the long distances involved in deployment on maneuvers or in any crosscountry flight. The fragamentation of Europe into small geographical arenas apparently had obscured the potential range of small high-performance planes. When internal tankage was stipulated, however, design limitations on space and balance determined how much auxiliary fuel could be carried.

The influence of Douhet may have been felt in this respect, as well as in bombing concepts. Although Douhet postulated an independent air force with two functions, 135 offense and defense, the impact of bomber offensives was picked up and stressed by both the air power proponents and those who denied the possibility or the morality of total war. It appeared that most, if not all, senior air officers around the world at the end of World War I saw the tremendous potential of the aerial thrust beyond the line of surface forces. On the one hand, this tended to exaggerate the need for, and the potency of, the close tactical support role of aircraft. On the other hand, the long-range potential against all targets excited the interest in this country of the proponents of air power with little concern for defense or the role of the small fighter. In Europe, where all targets became vulnerable to moderately long–range raids, there was more concern for defense over a wide area to be obtained by use of fast maneuverable planes. But since this was all "internal" at short range, the interceptor was not considered a long-range striking force in its own right.

THE POTENCY OF AIRCRAFT

An elaborate thesis can be developed to explain how different interpretations of the potency of aircraft in varied roles led each country to assign different priorities to aircraft development. In reverse, the priorities indicated collective thinking and national points of view.

In Germany, geographic conquest was a guiding principle that led to concentration upon offensive short-range aircraft. Fighters assumed a secondary role but were needed for defense. Performance was important, but range was not.

In England, with its reliance upon sea power, aerial defense of the home base was a top priority, and development in the mid-1930s reflected this.

In the United States, the Navy and Air Corps worked in two different ways. While positions and changes in policy as complex as procurement and national defense cannot be completely explained, a theory that fits the case can be suggested to help explain how decisions affecting aircraft development might have been made.

A naval force represents a complete mobile base with its own offensive and defensive capabilities. Although it does need resupply, it is logistically self-sufficient for a fairly long period of time. Not surprisingly, the first extension of aircraft was as scouting adjuncts to surface ships. Next, torpedo-carrying and dive-bombing planes were developed; they were longer-range versions of naval surface weapons except that they carried bombs instead of heavy shells. Intense anti-aircraft fire from the surface ships provided defense. As the potency of aircraft attack against ships was recognized as serious enough to justify using aircraft defensively, the ship-based fighter on aircraft carriers became an integral part of a task force. But the carrier could accommodate longer-range offensive types, as well. By evolution, the carrier thus became the focus of a striking task force.

Because the surface vessel moved as a base into fairly close proximity to the point of attack for the air group, the aircraft on it were naturally short- to mid-range. The natural restrictions of handling aircraft on a carrier also restricted the size. Catapults, arresting gear, elevators, and working space made dimensions and weight critical items.

Generally speaking, the planes developed for naval use were similar in size and performance to equivalent land-based types. Special detail-design considerations were necessary for operating from a deck. These included arresting gear hooks, special criteria for landing gears, and more attention to lateral control on slow-speed approaches, plus folding wings on the larger aircraft to permit closer stacking on deck.

More significant than the planes themselves was the relative ease with which inevitable conflicts between ground control of aircraft and independent action were reconciled. The aviators lived and operated from the ship, whose mission was to occupy a certain spot and to exert pressure both from its presence and from its striking ability. The naval surface commanders naturally used the enhanced capability provided by air for both offense and defense. The task force commander could be an airman. There might have been serious differences of opinion within the service about the real effectiveness of airplanes, but there appeared to be little question of the acceptance of air as an inherent adjunct of surface naval force. The growing appropriations for naval air all during the prewar period but particularly in the early 1930s substantiated this conclusion.

If the integration of air with surface force was relatively easy in the Navy, it was not so in the Army. Apparently, President Roosevelt not only appreciated the naval situation but also believed (as many other people did) that air could be similarly meshed with ground operations. As late as 1940 he was publicly referring to air as an integral part of the surface force and surface struggle.

The ground situation was relatively nonmobile, which meant that range to distant targets had to be provided in the aircraft themselves. The Navy had long-range shore-based aircraft, flying boats, and dirigibles, but this function was always a small part of the total and was largely used for offshore scouting. In the Army, ground commanders wanted to *see* the aircraft in the battle zone and to use the scouting function in close proximity to the ground troops, as it had been in World War I.

Defense, to the Army ground commander, meant keeping enemy air forces from inflicting casualties and interfering with friendly internal, behind-the-lines activities. He had little interest in anything on the enemy side of the lines except interdicting the supply and reinforcement of enemy ground troops.

During the early part of the prewar period, there were two-seater observation and attack airplanes that were about the same size as the D.H.4 and designed to perform about the same mission. By the mid-1930s, the potential for all sizes and types of aircraft had increased with the advances in technology. Nevertheless, the gap between potential and reality was extensive, because of all the adverse circumstances previously discussed.

For the mid-size aircraft, there was some extension beyond the 0-1, 0-2, 0-38, and the attack A-3, A-8, A-12, A-17. The observation types went as far as the 0-47,

Experience with the Curtiss A-18 Shrike proved the advantages of twin-engined attack planes and established Air Corps requirements that eventually resulted in the Douglas A-20 and A-26 designs.

which provided for an observer's position in a guppy belly below the wing. Curtiss built a twin-engine attack plane, or light bomber, the A-18, which presaged the light to medium bombers that became the short-range interdiction craft. Douglas's A-20, several of which were procured, and the later A-26 were natural follow-on types. But the close support role of a special type began to disappear as fighter capability and weight-carrying ability developed. The fighter-bomber became a recognized form, although this was specifically prohibited as a fighter function in the mid-1930s.

There had been large bombers in World War I, and Douhet, in writing up to 1929, had described what became known as strategic bombing. Although Douhet appeared to be a spokesman for new aerial concepts, there were airmen all over the world who foresaw the air as a new ocean to be navigated, exploited, and defended. General Mitchell became the champion of air attack, but the tests against the battleships in 1922 were more generally interpreted to be isolated tests of the relative vulnerability of ships to aerial bombing. Most senior airmen in this country saw these tests as just one instance of the increasing capability of aircraft. They were waiting for further technical development to provide the means to demonstrate the full potential of air power.

COMMAND AND EMPLOYMENT

After 1934, as aircraft and power plant development gave assurance of much increased performance, many of the conflicts over command and employment grew from mere subjects of discussion into real problems. Each level of command of ground forces wanted aircraft assigned to its command to further its own limited objectives. The range and mobility of planes permitted employment over areas larger than those assigned to small units. Allocation to ground units tended to fragment the force and to prevent the concentration of whatever few planes might be available. The problem simply was determining the proper level of command at which coordination should be achieved. As the war developed, this level became the theater command for the long-range force.

General Foulois had succeeded in his tour as chief in getting recognition of a GHQ (General Headquarters) Air Force. But it was several years before this organization became a reality. Maneuvers of the 1930s had worked out some of the mechanics of coordinated action. The British in the Battle of Britain and in the night fighter defense developed GCI (Ground Controlled Intercept), which established the form of coordination and the "real time" direction of the air forces involved. As this mechanism developed, the control centers for close tactical support with representatives of all units concerned tended to eliminate the problems. Nevertheless, control remains a sticky question in the 1980s.

In the 1930s, "control" meant more than the allocation and direction of forces in being. It also dictated policy for development and priority for procurement. This was the aspect that contributed to the difficulty of building an adequate posture before 1939.

As the prospect for obtaining a bombing force with a long-range mission (later called strategic) developed, the bombing doctrine left the fighters behind as a purely defensive effort. The bombers envisioned heavy defensive armament and mutual support of firepower in formations precluding the need for fighters. As the range of fighters increased, the possibility of using fighters as an adjunct of the bombing thrust arose and a peculiar inconsistency developed. The bombers, having succeeded in releasing the air strike from supervision of the surface force while engaging in offensive operations, now developed a doctrine of tieing the fighter to

North American broke new ground in 1937 with its 0-47 observation planes by building a three-man aircraft, larger and heavier than older observation types. It relocated the observer's station in the belly for a view unobstructed by the wing.

the bombers in a close-support defensive role. This tended to restrict the inherent mobility and offensive character of the fighters. Only as the war expanded were the fighters used more freely to attain air superiority.

"Air superiority," "mastery of the air," and "command of the air" were typical phrases that had been used in various forms since before World War I. As concepts, they were too intangible for use as doctrines of development or employment. The offensive aspect realized that an aerial attack could be pressed home regardless of opposition, if it was worth the cost. But this cut both ways since the enemy could also achieve this. Indeed, the kamikaze attack against naval vessels may represent the ultimate version of this concept. On the other hand, aerial defense could exact such a penalty that attacks could not be continued very long. Since aircraft could not occupy territory or retain target areas, it became a matter of exerting pressure that influenced the decisions made by command. In the last analysis, what was implied was simply the *relative* freedom to use the air both for offense and defense, compared to the enemy's freedom to use it for his own purposes. Since the ocean of air goes down to the ground, the relative freedom of the air also determined the relative freedom to operate on the surface, both at the point of contact and deep in home territory.

To exploit this principle fully, it has to be recognized that the whole spectrum of types and performance of aircraft must be utilized for there to be success. Preoccupation with one aspect artificially restricts the full utilization of an inherent capability and permits choices by an enemy that could otherwise be denied. This happened with our fighter doctrine, and the fighter almost died as a dynamic concept in the United States. Having no home defense mission as an urgent requirement, and being limited to supplementing ground activity and accompanying bombers at short range, fighters were kept alive by a small number of enthusiasts. This was partly a love of the maneuverable plane, partly a feeling for the fighter's inherent value when it was used fully, and partly a recognition of the technical possibilities for greatly enhancing its performance with advances in technology. Whatever the motivation, the fighter was kept alive, but at a low priority.

The Air Corps could exploit increases in wing loading more easily than the Navy could. Increases in weight itself simply involved slightly longer ground rolls on takeoff and better brakes on landing. On the carriers, there was the problem of catapult capacity and higher minimum speeds. Thus, in the days of the biplane, there were Army and Navy types, particularly fighter types, that were substantially identical in both services, Curtiss Hawks and Boeing P-12s and F4Bs. With the advent of the higher wing loading land-based planes, there was a diversion of the trend of development in the two services.

The "Droop-Snoot," a Lockheed P-38 with field modification, was equipped to carry a bombardier and a Norden bombsight.

To appreciate the impact of the appearance of Allied fighters over Berlin and deep into Russia, it is necessary to see what happened technically in the mid-1930s. By being so subtle that it escaped recognition, the progress was almost sneaky. First, efficiency in lift versus drag increased tremendously in the pursuit of ever-increasing high speed, which meant that longer and longer ranges were possible. This prospect was never exploited, however, because of the needs for allocating a large part of the maximum lifting capability, to increased armament loads and for structural strength for violent maneuvering at high speed. High speed also dictated lower power loadings, i.e., more and more power for the weight involved. The final input was the matter of weight itself. While all fighters, or, more properly, high-power maneuverable planes, had always had the ability to exploit overload, fuel capacity was never very large in lightweight machines. Further, the high drag of biplanes, for instance, meant that no attainable increase in fuel capacity added much to the range. These factors applied in varying degrees to all sizes and types; they just happened to be more impressive in the small sizes and, at the same time, less well recognized.

Perhaps, no tactical scenario had been developed during peacetime while the changes were taking place that demonstrated a need for a long-range capability. In fact, as has been indicated, there was some opposition to making any excursions into this area. Their reluctance stemmed largely from the frustration of trying to get competitive performance in inventory planes. But in 1940, when the developing war in Europe began to indicate the need for long-range ferrying flight, the informal relationships between the services and the industry made getting technical investigations started possible, despite the injunctions prohibiting their application.

The results are well known. Lockheed, guided by designer Kelly Johnson and pilot Milo Burcham, demonstrated that the P-28's range was still 2,200 miles when two 150-gallon tanks were carried on its bomb racks and better than 3,000 miles with two 300-gallon tanks. These modifications were quickly adapted to the other fighters with differing arrangements and capacities. The internal bullet-protected tankage had, incidentally, increased the combat radius, even without the external fuel, well beyond the maximum range that had been figured necessary for the mid-1930s.

The flexibility of these arrangements was soon utilized in combat. A load of 150 gallons of fuel and its tank translated into about 1,000 pounds, which could alternatively be a 1,000-pound bomb. The 300-gallon tanks could be replaced with a 2,000-pound bomb. Fuel and bombs could be used in differing combinations. Reports from the Pacific indicated that one 300-gallon tank was used for range extension, while the plane's other bomb rack pylon was used to carry a bomb. In Europe, shorter-range flights were made with P-38s carrying two 2,000-pound bombs plus either full machine gun and cannon armament or a bombardier and bombsight in the "droop snoot." When it is considered that the 4,000-pound bomb load was the same as the "design point" load of the B-17, it can be seen that it would have been difficult indeed to forecast this as a requirement at the time the aircraft was initiated.

The larger sizes had, of course, access to the same technical progress. There had been corresponding utilization of long-range ferry tanks in the bomb bays, and overload was just as drastically exploited. However, with the lower proportion of weight in the structural elements of the relatively nonmaneuverable bombers and with the higher power loadings, the additions were less dramatic. It was always expected that the big airplanes would carry heavy loads for long distances; so the increases due to technical development were accepted almost without comment. In addition, the ultimate desires in load and range were always moving ahead of realization so that due credit was rarely given to what was actually happening.   141

NEW OPPORTUNITIES

As the performance and flexibility of employment increased, the option available to operators and commanders expanded, and the choices became more difficult. Personnel entering the service just before the war found these characteristics already in being and accepted them as part of learning the operational ropes. They had some difficulty with techniques but little with concept. Most of the older operators, who were masters of technique, adapted readily, but there were still occasional misunderstandings. A junior group commander in the Philippines was ordered early in the war to bomb a target at long range. He explained that he could carry the bombs but could not carry enough fuel to return over water to base. Or he could go to the target and return but without bombs. The senior chose not to expend the force for a doubtful target, but the junior was close to being accused of refusing a mission.

In the history of war, there are always incidents where individuals leave their imprint and somehow predetermine an event's outcome. In the bigger picture, which involves all the forces, their training, and equipping, it is more difficult to recognize the individual contributions. The results record their participation, even though their names may not be famous.

One group that definitely left its signature on the planet was the test pilots. The companies had their development and production test pilots. The military had engineering and operational development test pilots. The NACA had its own test pilots. In the time being considered, test pilots carried the tradition of good and safe handling qualities and imprinted their individual preferences on the machines with which they worked.

Another group, production managers, who were sometimes vice presidents, were the individuals who established the facilities that permitted the engineers to translate ideas into reality. The ruggedness and reliability that made superior weapons were the results of a happy union of engineering and manufacturing skill. Harry H. Wezel of Douglas was highly respected in the industry in the 1930s and was an indispensable part of the team that made the company so important a factor. Pete Jensen at Curtiss was a dominant figure in the company and undoubtedly was largely responsible for Curtiss's performance.

Not all the people prominent in the early days managed to survive the perils of rapid expansion. There were those whose contributions had been significant in the smaller scale of activity who found themselves temperamentally unsuited for the housekeeping and personnel management chores of tremendously expanded operations.

There were many, however, who entered the field after 1927 and who adapted and rode the tide during the 1930s to positions of ever-increasing responsibility. Many junior military pilots quickly became unit commanders and distinguished themselves. There was, for example, Curtis E. LeMay, who was in the group qualified for instrument landings during the mail operation. Later, he set some records with the OA-5, the large Douglas Amphibian. During the war, he commanded the Second Bomb Wing and led the Regensburg Raid. After the war, he commanded the Strategic Air Command and became chief of staff of the Air Force.

No record of the tenuous and uncertain period of the 1930s is complete without full credit being given to the part played by Oliver Echols. From 1934 to 1940, he was chief engineer and then assistant chief of the matériel division at Wright Field. During this time, he was the key figure in the initiation of all the weapons that became available for the dramatic expansion of production. In 1940, he was transferred to headquarters in Washington. After that, he had a number of titles, though all of them added up to the same job. For the last two years of the war, he was assistant chief of air staff for matériel, maintenance, and distribution. As such, he was responsible for the development, procurement, logistic support, and delivery of weapons.

Although the Navy maintained a development and procurement program of its own, many of the airplane and engine companies benefited from the efforts of Echols; and since many of them supplied both the Air Corps and the Navy, his impact was felt outside the Air Corps development and procurement system. He was a key figure in the negotiations with our allies, before we entered the war, that helped to overcome our unpreparedness. It would have been hard to find a more highly trusted and respected man in the whole aircraft field. After the war, a measure of the esteem in which the industry held him was indicated by his appointment as president of the Aircraft Industries Association.

The air battles in Europe raged over the battlefield of Crécy. One year short of 600 years after the famous battle, a new weapon, the airplane, was crucial in the victory. Supposedly, the longbow had been developed over hundreds of years, while the airplane reached its level of proficiency in a scant forty. But providing the weapons of 1940 to 1945 depended more on the men and women who participated than on the characteristics of the weapons themselves. Without the few people involved, the weapons would have been different, and the battles themselves would have been different. Perhaps 600 years from World War II, history will draw more significant conclusions about the survival of the Free World than some superficial assessment that planes were better than ground soldiers. The ground soldiers and the planes were there when needed, and it was no magic that provided the means through which air power came of age.

INDEX

Italicized page numbers refer to illustrations.

between the wars, 48–50, 71; range
considerations, 64, 65. *See also specific B-type
aircraft listings*
Bombers, light, 24, 72, 138
Bombs, 63
Bombsights, 63
Brakes, 81
Bristol Bullet monoplane, 75
Britain. *See* England
Broadhurst, Harry, 134
Browning machine guns, 59, 62
BT-2 aircraft, 103
Bullets, 62
Burcham, Milo, 68, 141
Buying Aircraft (Holley), 108

C-1 aircraft, 109
C-47 aircraft, 57, 77
C-54 aircraft, 119
Caldwell, Frank, 84
California Institute of Technology, 34
Cannon, Joseph A., 93
Cannons, 60, 62
Caproni bombers, 48
Cargo aircraft. *See* Transport aircraft; *specific C-type
aircraft listings*
Carriers, 25, 40, 52, 136, 139–40
Cessna Aircraft Co., Inc., 21, 94
Chamberlin, Clarence, 103
Change orders, 119–22
Chester, Arthur, 44
Civil Aeronautics Act, 32
Civilian aviation: airmail contracts, 34–36, 38–39,
100, 101, 103–6; early activities, 33–35;
passenger and mail transport developments, 35–37
Civilian Conservation Corps, 44
Clipper aircraft, 36, 78
Coffin, Howard E., 32, 33
Collier Trophy, 30, 84
Colt's Patent Firearms Co., 60, 62
Commerce Department, 105
Commercial aviation. *See* Civilian aviation
Competitions, design, 108–10, 119
Concurrent spares, 20
Condor aircraft, 78, 109, 110
Congressional Aviation Policy Board, 15
Conqueror engine, 29, 31
Consolidated Aircraft Corp., 36, 51, 93
Construction materials, 28
Cooling systems, 28–31
Cover, Carl, 14, 82, 93
Crécy, battle of, 124, 143
Curtis, Edward P., 126
Curtiss, Glenn H., 92
Curtiss Condor aircraft, 78, 109, 110
Curtiss D-12 engine, 29, 30
Curtiss Falcons, 66, *67*
Curtiss Hawk biplane, 66, 82, 140
Curtiss Lark biplane, 35
Curtiss-Wright Conqueror engine, 29, 31
Curtiss-Wright Corp., 15, 20, 34, 50, 66, 69–70,
77–78, 82, 84, 93, 94, 109, 126, 127, 142

D.I aircraft, *76*
D. VII aircraft, 75, 77, 78, 90, 126
D-12 engine, 29, 30
Damon, Ralph, 125–26
Dayton Wright Co., 78
DB-1 aircraft, 86
DC aircraft series, 58
DC-2 aircraft, 78, 81, 86, 101, 109, 110
DC-3 aircraft, 37, 86, 120
DC-4 aircraft, 93, 119
de Havilland Aircraft Co., Ltd., 89
Denmark, 62
Deperdussin fighter, 90
Design competitions, 108–9, 119
Design drawings, 113
DGA aircraft, 44
D.H.4 aircraft, *34,* 35, 36, 48, *49,* 50, 77, 78, 84, 85
Diamond, Harry, 38
Doolittle, James H., 13, 38, 41, 93, 103, 127
Douglas Aircraft Co., Inc., 34, 37, 50, 78, 82, 93,
109, 110, 127, 142
Douhet, Giulio, 46, 135–36, 138
Douhet theory, 46–47, 65

Eaker, Ira C., 127
Echols, Oliver, 45, 68, 142–43
Eisenhower, Dwight D., 92, 126
Ely, Eugene, 92
Engines. *See* Aircraft engines
England, 17, 22, 30, 47, 58–60, 62, 78, 124, 136
Ethylene glycol, 30, 31
Experimental aircraft. *See specific X-type and Y-type
aircraft listings*

F-3F aircraft, 81
F-4B aircraft, 52, 66, 140
F4B-1 aircraft, *53*
F-5L flying boat, 36
Fairchild, Sherman, 33
Fairchild Aircraft Div., 21, 109
FB-5a aircraft, *18*
Fighter aircraft: design development, 25, 56, 71, 72;
engine requirements, 58; functions of, 25,
138–41; gun configuration for, 59–60;
performance specifications, 58, 87, 132; propeller
design, 84; range considerations, 65–69, 135;
wing area, 89–90. *See also specific F-type and P-
type aircraft listings*
Fighter-bombers, 25, 138
Fire-control systems, 63
Fleet, Reuben, 93, 127
Float planes, 25
FM-1 aircraft, 55, 60, 85
Fokker, Anthony, 75
Fokker Aircraft Factory, 78
Fokker Trimotors, 36
Fokker Universals, 36
Ford Trimotors, 36, 37, 117
Foulois, Benjamin D., 39, 41, 127, 138
Fowler flap, 115
France, 22, 29, 62, 124
Fuel: and range considerations, 65–69, 135, 141

145

147